Creature Comforts: Poetic Animal Tales

Table of Contents

The Adventures of an Explorer Hamster

There once was a hamster named Harold,
Whose curiosity knew no bounds.
He was always on the lookout,
For new adventures to be found.
He had a little red wagon,
That he'd pack with all his gear.
And then he'd set off on his travels,
Without a single worry or fear.
He roamed through fields and forests,
And climbed up rocky cliffs.
He crossed rivers and streams,
And braved the darkest rifts.
He saw wonders beyond measure,
And had adventures grand.
But no matter where he roamed,
His little red wagon was always in hand.
So, if you ever see a hamster,
Roaming through the land,
Don't be afraid to say hello,
To Harold, the explorer hamster grand.

The Adventures of the Galactic Guinea Pig

There once was a guinea pig named Gus,
Who lived a life full of fuss.
He was a restless little fellow,
And he had a heart full of hollow.
One day, he decided to leave it all behind,
And go on an adventure of the most grand kind.
He hopped on a rocket ship and blasted off into space,
Leaving behind his mundane life at this place.
As he soared through the galaxy,
He saw sights that took his breath away.
He visited planets of all shapes and sizes,
And met creatures both strange and wise.
But no matter where his journey took him,
Gus never lost his adventurous spirit.
He roamed the stars with curiosity and glee,
And had the time of his life, as you can see.
So, if you ever feel the urge to break free,
Just remember the tale of Gus the guinea pig,
And let your adventurous spirit roam,
For the galaxy is full of wonders to be shown.

The Curious case of the Capybara Detective
The curious case of the capybara detective,
A rodent of great renown,
With a nose for clues and a mind so sharp,
He was the best in the rodent town.
He wore a trench coat and a fedora,

And carried a magnifying glass,
As he prowled the streets in search of clues,
He moved with stealth and class.
He solved crimes that others could not,
And always got his man,
For he was clever and determined,
And as quick as he was wan.
But despite his success and fame,
He was still just a humble rat,
Content to live in his burrow,
And solve mysteries where're he's at.
So, if you ever need a detective,
And the case is just too tough,
Call on the capybara,
He'll sniff out the evidence and such.

The Epic Quest of Samurai Kitty

The epic quest of Samurai Kitty,
A feline hero, sleek as can be,
With stealth and precision, she roamed the city,
A true expert in the art of the sneak
With her sword by her side, sharp as a knife,
She battled the rats and the mice,
Defending her territory with honor and might,
And earning the respect of her tribe.
But her quest was not just one of battle,
For a true samurai must also seek wisdom,
So, she traveled to distant lands and mettle,
To learn the ways of the world and the kingdom.
Through her trials and tribulations,
She grew stronger and more wise,
And in the end, she emerged victorious,
A true samurai in fur and eyes.
Now she sits upon her throne,
A ruler of all she surveys,
A symbol of courage and strength,
And a true warrior in all her ways.

The Nine Lives of Kung Fu Cat

The nine lives of Kung Fu Cat,
A feline warrior with skills so fine,
With a heart of courage and a spirit so bold,
He's a master of the martial art divine.
He trains hard and practices his craft,
With a focus and determination,
His moves are swift and deadly,
A true inspiration.
He faces every challenge,
With a fierce and fearless grace,
For he knows that with each life,
Comes a new test to face.
But with each life he gains,
Comes a new lesson learned,
And with each victory,
His skill and wisdom earned.
The nine lives of Kung Fu Cat,
May come to an end one day,
But his legacy will live on,
In the hearts of those who learned to train and play

The Friendly Giraffe's Necktie Party

There once was a giraffe named Gerry
Whose neck was long and very hairy
He loved to dress up with style
And always had a grin that was quite a while
One day, he had an idea so grand
A necktie party, in his savannah land
He invited all his animal friends
To come and make amends
They gathered round with ties so neat
Bright colors, patterns, oh so sweet
The zebras had stripes, the lions' spots
Even the birds wore fancy ties with knots
Gerry was the host with the most
His necktie was polka dots
They ate, they danced, they sang
Until the stars twinkled and rang
It was a party to remember
With friends and ties, it was a true treasure
And from that day on, every year
Gerry's necktie party was the animal's cheer

Silly Sally the Squirrel

Silly Sally the squirrel, so funny and spry
Loved to play in the trees, way up high
She'd climb and jump, with acorn in hand
Making her friends laugh, throughout the land
She'd slide down branches, with a giggle and a grin
Fluffy tail waving, as she tumbled within
She'd play hide and seek, with her squirrel crew
Making everyone laugh, with her antics anew
One day, she found a nut, so big and round
She couldn't wait to show it off, she bounded
But as she scampered down the tree
She slipped and fell, oh dear me!
But Sally, being the silly one
Landed on her feet, with a laugh and a bun
She picked up her nut, and scampered away
Making her friends laugh, until the end of the day
Silly Sally, the squirrel, so full of fun
Made every day an adventure, for everyone
She taught them to laugh, to play and to be
Silly and happy, just like her, wild and free.

Greg the Giraffe's Great Adventure

Greg the giraffe, with legs so tall
Wanted to see the world, one and all
He dreamed of adventures, far and wide
And decided to take a journey, with pride
He set out on his journey, with a spring in his step
The savannah was his home, but he wanted to explore, to be adept
He traveled through the jungle, and the desert too
He met new animals, and learned a thing or two
He saw the lions, who were fierce and strong
He saw the elephants, who sang a song
He saw the monkeys, who swung from tree to tree
He even saw the ocean, as far as the eye could see
He had many adventures, and many tales to tell
Of all the things he saw, and all the things he smelled
He returned home, with a heart full of joy
And shared his stories, with every girl and boy
Greg the giraffe, with legs so tall
Had a great adventure, after all.

The Clever Fox and the Grapes

There once was a clever little fox
Who loved to play and explore, like a clock
He roamed the woods, in search of a treat
And one day, he came across a grape vine, so sweet
The grapes were plump and juicy, red, and ripe
But they were high up, beyond his reach, a real gripe
He tried to jump, but it was no use
The grapes were too high, and he couldn't choose
But being clever, as foxes are
He came up with a clever plan, from afar
He looked at the grapes, and said with a grin
"They're probably sour, I wouldn't want them, I'll win"
So, he walked away, with his tail held high
Pretending he didn't want them, and let out a sigh
The grapes, he knew, were out of his reach
But his clever mind, had made him a winner, a beach
The moral of the story, is simple to see
Sometimes, what we want, might not be what we need, it's key.

Mary the Mouse and the Cheese Thief

Mary the mouse, lived in a cozy little house
With her family, she shared all her cheese
But one day, a thief, brought her to her knees
The thief stole all her cheese, in the middle of the night
Leaving Mary and her family, without any bite
But Mary being clever, as mice often are
Decided to catch the thief, near or far
She set a trap, with cheese as the bait
And waited for the thief, to fall for her fate
The thief came back, as she knew he would
And got caught in her trap, as he should
Mary was able to retrieve all her cheese
And the thief was caught, with ease
She shared her cheese, with her family and friends
And the thief was never seen again
Mary the mouse, showed that being small
Does not mean, you can't catch a thief, after all.

Guinea Pig Mayhem

In a cozy little cage, lived three guinea pigs
They were happy and content, wiggling their wigs
But one day, something went awry
And the guinea pigs caused a mayhem, oh my!
They gnawed their way through the bars
And made a break for the stars
They ran through the house, with squeals and squeaks
Leaving a trail of hay, and making the humans freaks
They rolled in the carpet, and ate the plants
They even took a nap, on the windowsills, and chants
The humans chased them, around and around
But the guinea pigs, were too fast, and had found
A way to have fun, and enjoy their day
They caused a little mayhem, but in a playful way
In the end, the humans couldn't help but smile
At the silly little guinea pigs, causing chaos, all the while.

On the Range with Cowboy Ferret

Out on the range, where the cactus grow
Lived a cowboy ferret, named Joe
He wore a hat, and boots to match
And carried a lasso, that he could attach
He rode his trusty steed, a prairie dog
Through the dusty plains, like a true cowboy, a slog
He chased after varmints, and cattle too
With a ferret's determination, he knew what to do
He slept under the stars, with his bedroll tight
Woke up at dawn, to start a new fight
He sang cowboy songs, as he rode along
And dreamed of finding, a prairie song
But one day, his prairie dog got spooked
By a snake, and Joe was thrown, like he was hooked
He landed in a cactus, and got stuck
But he didn't let that, make him out of luck
He used his lasso, to pull himself free
And got back on his feet, as wild as can be
He continued on his journey, with a smile
On the range, with cowboy ferret, Joe, all the while.

Super Spy Chipmunk

Deep in the forest, where the trees sway
Lived a chipmunk, who was an expert at play
He was small and fast, with a keen eye
And a talent for espionage, that could not be denied
He had a secret lair, deep in the ground
Filled with gadgets and gizmos, that made a profound
He donned a suit, and a trench coat too
And set out on his mission, with nothing to do
He spied on the animals, and gathered information
He cracked codes, and foiled plans, with determination
He saved the day, from the shadow's unseen
With his quick wit, and his chipmunk gleam
He was the super spy, that no one knew
But when danger struck, he always came through
He protected the forest, with stealth and skill
And kept his secret identity, safe and still
So, if you're ever in the forest, and you hear a sound
Don't be surprised, if you see a chipmunk, around
It might just be the super spy at work
Keeping the forest, safe and free, like a perk.

The Lazy Bear's Picnic

The lazy bear lay on his back
In the warm sunshine, snacking on a snack
He munched on honey, berries, and bread
And lazily scratched his furry head
He thought of all the things he'd do
When he finally got up, but for now it was just too
Nice to lay there and soak up the sun
This was the life, this was fun
But then he heard a rustling in the trees
He opened one eye to see what it could be
A group of animals, with baskets in hand
Were headed towards his picnic land
The bear groaned and rolled on his side
He didn't want to share his spot, but couldn't decide
To be rude and chase them away
So, he just lay there, and let them stay
They spread out their blankets and sat down to eat
The bear's stomach growled; he couldn't help but cheat
A peek at their food, it looked so delicious
He couldn't resist, he had to join in, auspicious
The animals welcomed him with open arms
And the bear enjoyed the feast, free from qualms
He realized that sharing is indeed
A great way to enjoy a picnic indeed
And so, the lazy bear lay back
With a full belly, a smile on his face
Content in the company, in the sun so bright
This was the perfect lazy bear's picnic alright.

Sailor Otter's Odyssey

Anchors aweigh, the sailor otter cried
As he set sail on the ocean wide
With a grin on his face and a song in his heart
He knew this journey was going to start
The wind in his fur, the salt on his face
He felt alive in this wild and free place
He danced on the deck and swam in the sea
This was where he was meant to be
He navigated the waves with ease
And sang to the dolphins and whales as they breeze
He fished for his dinner and slept under the stars
Living life as a sailor, without any bars
But as the journey came to an end
He knew he'd be back, again and again
To the sea and the wind and the endless horizon
This was where he belonged, his true dominion
Anchors aweigh, the sailor otter cried
As he set sail on the ocean wide
With a grin on his face and a song in his heart
He knew this journey was just the start.

A Busy Beaver's Bakery

The busy baker beaver was in a hurry
As she mixed and measured in a flurry
Flour, sugar, eggs, and milk
She had to make the cake before the ilk
She beat the batter with a wooden spoon
Humming a tune, in her baking boon
She poured it into a pan with care
Making sure it was spread out fair
Into the oven, it went with a whistle
She set the timer, and began to thistle
She tidied up her kitchen space
As she waited for the perfect cake
The smell of baking filled the air
It was a scent beyond compare
Finally, the timer went off with a beep
The cake was done, she let out a leap
She took it out, and let it cool
Then frosted it with a vanilla drool
She decorated it with berries and nuts
It looked so beautiful, she couldn't put
She cut a slice, and took a bite
It was delicious, everything was right
The busy baker beaver was pleased
With her masterpiece, her heart was appeased.

The Singing Elephant's Trunk

The singing elephant raised his trunk high
As he sang a melody to the sky
His deep, rumbling voice echoed far and wide
Filling the hearts of all who heard it with pride
He sang of love and loss, of hope and fear
His words touched the hearts of those who were near
He sang of the beauty of the wild
And of the importance of being reconciled
His trunk was his instrument, his voice
With it, he could make the most beautiful noise
He swayed and trumpeted, as he sang his song
His trunk swaying along
The other animals stopped to listen
To the singing elephant's trunk, glisten
They were mesmerized by his voice
And the emotions that he evoked
The singing elephant sang till the end
Till the stars came out, and the moon rose again
And as the night grew dark and the stars came out
The singing elephant's trunk sang, a song of no doubt
His music was a reminder of the beauty of life
And the importance of appreciating the strife
And even when the singing elephant was gone
His songs and legacy would live on.

The Dancing Flamingo's Shoes

The dancing flamingo stood tall and proud
With her pink feathers, she stood out in the crowd
She wore a pair of shoes, bright and red
They were the perfect accessory for her bed
She twirled and dipped, on her long legs
To the beat of the music, she moved with such grace and beg
Her shoes tapped and clacked, as she danced
She was the life of the party, in a trance
The other animals watched in awe
As the dancing flamingo, danced without a flaw
She moved with such elegance, poise, and style
She made everyone else, seem quite vile
But as the night went on, and the party was winding down
The dancing flamingo's shoes, began to make a frown
She could feel her feet, aching and sore
She knew she couldn't dance, anymore
But even as she took off her shoes
And her feet cried out, the blues
She knew that the memories, would last
Of the dancing flamingo, and her shoes from the past
For the dancing flamingo, shoes were more than just footwear
They were a symbol of her passion, her art, and her lure
And even as she retired for the night
The memory of her dancing would still be bright.

The Grumpy Gorilla's Good Day

The grumpy gorilla woke up one day
Feeling grouchy, in every single way
He grumbled and groaned, as he got out of bed
And wished that he could just stay in bed
He stumbled to the kitchen, with a scowl
And made himself a cup of coffee, to make him feel whole
But it was too hot, and too bitter
Making his grumpiness, even more bitter
He went outside, to take a walk
But the sun was too bright, and the birds sang too much talk
He wanted peace and quiet, but all he got
Was the sound of the leaves, rustling a lot
He went back inside, and sat on his couch
He was determined, to have a grouchy day, without a doubt
But then something strange happened, as he sat there
He felt a smile, tugging at the corners of his hair
He couldn't figure out what it was
But he felt a sudden warmth, in his heart because
He realized, that despite his grumpiness
He had a comfortable home, and a loving family's blessedness
So, he decided, to make the most of his day
And not let his bad mood, get in the way
He went outside, and took a deep breath
And felt the sun on his face, a new day's freshness
The grumpy gorilla, had a good day
And it was all because, he chose to make it that way.

The Lost Lamb's New Friends

The lost lamb wandered, through fields of green
With no one to guide her, she was just a teen
She bleated and called, for her mother and flock
But all she heard was silence, like a blocked clock
She felt alone and scared, in this new place
She missed the warmth, of her family's embrace
But then she heard a sound, that caught her ear
It was the distant bleating, of sheep she could hear
She followed the sound, with hope in her heart
And soon she came upon, a brand-new start
She found a new flock, and they welcomed her in
With open arms, and a smile, that could never be grim
The lost lamb was no longer lost
She had found a new family, at any cost
They taught her how to graze and play
And showed her the joys, of a new day
She learned to love, this new home
And was grateful, to no longer roam
The lost lamb had found, her new friends
And her heart was filled, with love that never ends.

The Brave Mouse's Big Rescue

The brave mouse, was small in size
But her courage, was larger than life's prize
She lived in the walls, of a grand old house
And knew every nook and cranny, like a spouse
One day, she heard a commotion
A cry for help, with a lot of motion
She followed the sound, to the kitchen floor
Where she found, a cat trapped behind a door
The mouse knew, she had to act fast
She couldn't let the cat, be trapped in the past
She scurried around, searching for a plan
And soon she had an idea, that was quite grand
She found a string, and tied it to a spoon
And with it, she managed to open the door soon
The cat was free, and so very grateful
And the mouse, felt her bravery, was now undeniable
The cat thanked the mouse, for her bravery and might
And the mouse felt, a surge of pride and delight
She may have been small, but her heart was big
And her rescue, was a story, that would always be a gig
The brave mouse had saved the day
And her courage, would forever stay.
The Wise Owl's Owl-some Advice
The wise owl sat on a branch high
His wise eyes, scanning the sky
He was known, for his owl-some advice
And his wisdom, was highly precise
The other animals, would often come
To seek his guidance when they were glum
They knew that the wise owl would know

Just what to say, and how to help them grow
He would listen, with a patient ear
To each of their problems, without any fear
Then he would speak, in a wise old tone
Sharing his wisdom, and helping them to hone
He would tell them, to be true to themselves
And to trust their instincts, without any wealth
He would remind them, that mistakes were okay
For it was through them, that they'd learn to play
The animals, left feeling uplifted and light
With the wise owl's owl-some advice, they felt alright
They knew that no matter what, the wise owl would be there
To guide them, with his wisdom and care
The wise owl, was more than just a bird
He was a friend, a mentor, a wise old word
And even though he was old, his advice was still new
For it was timeless, and always true.

The Bouncing Kangaroo's Big Jump

The bouncing kangaroo, was full of energy
With her strong legs, she could jump with ease
She spent her days, hopping and playing
In the fields, her joy was displaying
But there was one thing, that she wanted to do
A big jump, that she had never pursued
She had heard of a place, where the grass was so high
That she could jump, up to the sky
So, one day, she set out on her quest
With determination, she was at her best
She hopped and hopped, till she reached the place
And saw the grass, with a smile on her face
She took a deep breath, and prepared to jump
With all her might, she gave a thump
She soared through the air, with a joyful leap
And landed safely, with a happy peep
She looked up, and saw the sky
She had done it, she could fly
She hopped and jumped, with all her might
Feeling proud of her big jump's sight
The bouncing kangaroo, had done it at last
She had achieved her goal, and had surpassed
All her expectations, with her big jump
And it was a memory, she would always chump.

The Busy Bee's Honey Heist

The busy bee, was always on the go
With her wings a-flutter, she'd to and fro
Collecting nectar, from flower to flower
Building her honey, by the hour
She worked tirelessly, day and night
To gather the sweetest, most delicious bite
But one day, as she was flying back
She saw a bear, with a honey sack
The bear had taken, all her hard-earned honey
Leaving her hive, empty and sunny
The busy bee, was filled with ire
She couldn't let the bear, get away with this entire
So, she rallied her fellow bees
And together, they set out to seize
The stolen honey, from the bear's den
And bring it back, to the hive again
They buzzed and swarmed, around the bear
Startling him, and making him scared
He dropped the sack, and ran away
And the bees, reclaimed their honey that day
The busy bee, was proud and relieved
Her honey was safe, and she had achieved
Justice for her hive, and her hard work
And the bear, had finally learned to never to lurk
The busy bee's honey heist, was a success
And she had proven, that even the smallest can possess
The courage and determination, to take a stand
And protect what's important, in their own land.

The Curious Cat's Exploration

The curious cat, was always on the prowl
With her tail held high, she'd explore and scowl
She loved to wander, and discover new things
The world was her playground, with hidden rings
She'd climb the tallest trees, and leap from branch to branch
She'd swim in the streams, and catch fish in her trench
She'd explore the caves, and roam through the fields
She'd find new adventures, that never yield
She was always asking questions
And seeking new lessons
She was never satisfied, with what she knew
She wanted to learn, everything anew
One day, she came across a mysterious door
She couldn't resist, she had to explore
She pushed it open, and stepped inside
And found herself, on an incredible ride
It was a world, unlike any she'd seen
With vibrant colors, and creatures serene
She explored every inch, with wide-eyed wonder
And made friends, with the creatures under
The curious cat, had found her heart's desire
A world full of exploration, that never tires
And even though she eventually returned home
The memories of her journey, would forever roam
The curious cat, had found her true calling
In the world of exploration, she was enthralling
And she knew that there were still so many places
To be explored, and many new faces.

The Strong Hippo's Big Lift

The strong hippo, was known for his might
He could lift, with ease, the heaviest weight
He spent his days, training, and flexing
Showing off his strength, without any second guessing
But there was one thing, that he wanted to do
A big lift, that he had never pursued
He had heard of a log, that was so big
That it could only be lifted, by a hippo as big as a twig
So, one day, he set out on his quest
With determination, he was at his best
He found the log, and stared in awe
It was bigger than he had ever saw
He took a deep breath, and prepared to lift
With all his might, he gave a swift
He lifted the log, with a single heave
And held it up, with his strength's reprieve
He looked up, and saw the sky
He had done it, he could fly
He flexed his muscles, with all his might
Feeling proud of his big lift's sight
The strong hippo, had done it at last
He had achieved his goal, and had surpassed
All his expectations, with his big lift
And it was a memory, he would always keep
From that day forth, the strong hippo's fame spread far and wide
His incredible strength was known and respected by all who were
beside
He continued to push himself, lifting weights even greater than before
His pride in his strength was evident, as he showed it off without a
bore.

The Mischievous Monkey's Misadventures

The mischievous monkey, was always up to no good
With a twinkle in his eye, and a mischievous mood
He loved to play pranks, and cause a stir
Making the other animals, wish for a purr
He'd steal bananas, from the gorilla's stash
And cause chaos, with a well-timed dash
He'd swing from vine to vine, with glee
Leaving the other animals, to look and see
But his misadventures, often got him in trouble
As he found out, on the double
He'd get caught, and have to pay the price
For his monkey business, wasn't very nice
Despite the consequences, he couldn't change
His mischievous nature, was part of his range
He continued to play pranks, and have fun
Knowing that he was, just a mischievous one
But as he grew older, he realized
That his actions, had a bigger prize
He learned to use his mischief for good
And his misadventures, were not just understood
The mischievous monkey, had found his place
In the world of pranks, with a smile on his face
He used his wit and cunning, for the betterment of all
And his mischievous monkey nature, was no longer a fall.

The Musical Mouse's Big Band

The musical mouse, was a tiny thing
But she had a talent, for making music ring
She played the piano, with such grace
And her melodies, put a smile on every face
She played for the other animals, in the forest
Her music, was loved and cherished by all, at the best
But she dreamed of something, more grand
A big band, that would take a stand
So, one day, she set out to find
Other musicians, of all kinds
She searched high and low, near and far
Until she had gathered, a group of stars
They practiced and rehearsed, day and night
Until they had the perfect sound, just right
They played their first concert, under the stars
And the animals, were swept away by the bars
The musical mouse, had achieved her goal
A big band, that was more than whole
Her music, filled the forest with sound
And her band, was the talk of the town
From that day on, the musical mouse's band
Traveled and played, all over the land
Bringing joy and happiness, to all who heard
And their music, was always preferred
The musical mouse, had found her place
In the world of music, with a smile on her face
She had created something beautiful, and it was all thanks to her
dream
And the band, was a testament to the power of a mouse's musical
theme.

The Daring Dolphin's Deep Dive

The daring dolphin, was always up for a thrill
With a playful grin, and a sense of free will
She loved to swim, in the deep blue sea
Exploring the depths, with such glee
She'd dive down, to the ocean floor
And swim through the coral, with so much more
She'd leap through the waves, with a splash
And play with the other dolphins, in a dash
But there was one thing, that she wanted to do
A deep dive, that she had never pursued
She had heard of a place, where the water was so clear
That she could see, the mysteries that were near
So, one day, she set out on her quest
With determination, she was at her best
She swam and swam, till she reached the place
And saw the water, with a smile on her face
She took a deep breath, and prepared to dive
With all her might, she gave a jive
She soared through the water, with a graceful dive
And reached the depths, where few had thrived
She saw the most incredible things
And her heart, began to sing
She swam back to the surface, with a joyful leap
And shared her adventure, with her dolphin kin's keep
The daring dolphin, had done it at last
She had achieved her goal, and had surpassed
All her expectations, with her deep dive
And it was a memory, she would always keep alive.

The Sleepy Sloth's Big Snooze

The sleepy sloth, was always drowsy
With droopy eyes, and a bit of mossy
He loved to sleep, all day and night
In the safety of the trees, where it was just right
He'd hang from branches, with a snore
And nap through the day, forevermore
He'd wake up just in time, for a snack
And then return to his nap, with a rack
But there was one thing, that he wanted to do
A big snooze, that he had never pursued
He had heard of a place, where the trees were so tall
That he could sleep, for days and for all
So, one day, he set out on his quest
With a yawn, he was at his best
He climbed and climbed, till he reached the place
And saw the trees, with a smile on his face
He took a deep breath, and prepared to snooze
With a smile, he closed his eyes to muse
He slept through the day, and the night
And dreamed of the most incredible sights
He woke up refreshed, and full of energy
And set out to explore, the new scenery
He climbed to the top, of the tallest tree
And looked out at the world, with glee
The sleepy sloth, had done it at last
He had achieved his goal, and had surpassed
All his expectations, with his big snooze
And it was a memory, he would always choose.

The Adventurous Alligator's Swamp Safari

The adventurous alligator, loved to roam
Through the swamps and wetlands, his true home
He'd slide through the water, with such grace
And explore every inch, of this place
He'd hunt for fish, and hunt for prey
And bask in the sun, all day and play
But there was one thing, that he wanted to do
A swamp safari, that he had never pursued
He had heard of a place, where the swamps were so wild
That he could see, the wonders that were piled
So, one day, he set out on his quest
With curiosity, he was at his best
He swam and swam, till he reached the place
And saw the swamps, with a smile on his face
He explored the swamps, and saw exotic creatures
He saw the rarest birds, and the biggest alligators
He swam through the murky waters, and climbed the tall trees
He saw the most incredible things, and it was a treat to seize
He swam back to his home, with a joyful leap
And shared his adventure, with his gator kin to keep
The adventurous alligator, had done it at last
He had achieved his goal, and had surpassed
All his expectations, with his swamp safari
And it was a memory, he would always carry.

The Napping Lion's Big Roar

The napping lion, was always tired
With a mane of gold, and a sense of pride
He loved to nap, under the sun
And rest his head, till the day was done
He'd lay on the grass, with a snore
And nap through the day, forevermore
He'd wake up just in time, for a hunt
And then return to his nap, with a grunt
But there was one thing, that he wanted to do
A big roar, that he had never pursued
He had heard of a place, where the lions were so strong
That they could roar, all day long
So, one day, he set out on his quest
With determination, he was at his best
He walked and walked, till he reached the place
And saw the lions, with a smile on his face
He took a deep breath, and prepared to roar
With all his might, he let out a raw
The sound echoed through the land
And the other lions, raised their hand
He felt a surge of power and pride
He had done it; he had let out his side
He returned to his kingdom, with a joyful leap
And shared his achievement, with his lion kin to keep
The napping lion, had done it at last
He had achieved his goal, and had surpassed
All his expectations, with his big roar
And it was a memory, he would always store.

The Playful Penguin's Iceberg Jump

The playful penguin, was always in motion
With a waddle in her step, and an ocean's devotion
She loved to slide and play on the icy floes
And jump from iceberg to iceberg, as she goes
She'd dive in the water, with a splash
And swim with the fish, in a dash
But there was one thing, that she wanted to do
An iceberg jump, that she had never pursued
She had heard of a place, where the icebergs were so high
That she could jump, up to the sky
So, one day, she set out on her quest
With determination, she was at her best
She waddled and slide, till she reached the place
And saw the icebergs, with a smile on her face
She took a deep breath, and prepared to jump
With all her might, she gave a thump
She soared through the air, with a graceful leap
And landed safely, on the next one, with a peaceful sleep
She looked up, and saw the sky
She had done it, she could fly
She slid and jumped, with all her might
Feeling proud of her iceberg jump's sight
The playful penguin, had done it at last
She had achieved her goal, and had surpassed
All her expectations, with her iceberg jump
And it was a memory, she would always chump.

The Sneaky Snake's Secret Mission

The sneaky snake, was always on the move
With a sly grin, and a serpentine groove
He loved to slither, in the shadows and hide
And sneak up on his prey, with stealth and pride
He'd catch his dinner, with a flick of his tongue
And swallow it whole, with a silent thung
But there was one thing, that he wanted to do
A secret mission, that he had never pursued
He had heard of a treasure, hidden deep in the earth
That only the sneakiest snake, could uncover its worth
So, one day, he set out on his quest
With cunning, he was at his best
He slithered and crept, through the underbrush
Till he reached the spot, with a subtle hush
He dug and dug, with his tail
Until the treasure, was revealed without fail
He coiled around it, with a triumphant grin
And slithered away, with his secret win
He returned to his home, with his treasure in tow
And kept it hidden, from those who didn't know
He had accomplished his mission, with skill and grace
And the treasure, was now his to embrace.

The Lucky Elephant's Big Win

The lucky elephant, was always fortunate
With a trunk full of luck, and a spirit elated
He loved to play games, and have fun
And his luck always seemed to come
He'd win at cards, and win at dice
And his opponents would think it wasn't nice
But there was one thing, that he wanted to do
A big win, that he had never pursued
He had heard of a lottery, with a grand prize
That only the luckiest elephant, could realize
So, one day, he set out on his quest
With his luck on his side, he was at his best
He bought a ticket, with a gentle trunk
And waited for the draw, with a bit of hunk
The day of the draw, arrived with a roar
And the numbers were called, with a final score
And to his surprise, he had won the jackpot
The prize was his, without a doubt
He trumpeted with joy, and let out a cheer
He had done it; he had won it dear
He returned to his herd, with a joyful leap
And shared his luck, with his elephant kin to keep
The lucky elephant, had done it at last
He had achieved his goal, and had surpassed
All his expectations, with his big win
And it was a memory, he would always spin.

The Hungry Hippo's Big Feast

The hungry hippo, was always famished
With a big appetite, and a stomach that was always vanquished
He loved to eat, and eat a lot
His hunger could never be brought to a stop
He'd gobble down, grass and fruits
And splash in the water, as he hoots
But there was one thing, that he wanted to do
A big feast, that he had never pursued
He had heard of a place, where the food was so bountiful
That he could eat, until he was full
So, one day, he set out on his quest
With hunger, he was at his best
He walked and walked, till he reached the place
And saw the food, with a smile on his face
He took a deep breath, and prepared to feast
With all his might, he gave a beast
He ate and ate, until he couldn't anymore
And finally, he was satisfied, to the core
He looked around, and saw the other animal's stare
He had done it, he had eaten it all, with care
He waddled back to his home, with a joyful leap
And shared his feast, with his hippo kin to keep
The famished hippopotamus, had finally succeeded
He had attained his objective, and exceeded
All that he had hoped for, with his grand banquet
And it was a recollection, he would forever hold in contentment.

The Brave Bear's Campfire Tales

The Brave Bear sat by the fire's light,
Telling tales of adventure and might,
Of battles won and rivers crossed,
And the strength of the bear that never was lost.
He spoke of the mountains that he had climbed,
And the valleys where he had roamed,
Of the fish that he caught and the berries he ate,
And the friends he had made on his journey home.
He spoke of the courage that it took,
To face the storms and the wild,
And of the wisdom that he gained,
From the struggles of the child.
And as the fire flickered and danced,
The Bear's tales of courage and strength,
Reminded us of all of the power,
That lies within our own length.
So let us all take a lesson,
From the Brave Bear's campfire tales,
And remember to be courageous,
In the midst of life's travails.

The Cheerful Chimpanzee's Banana Party

The Cheerful Chimpanzee threw a party,
With bananas piled high,
He invited all his friends and family,
To come and dance and sing and sigh.
They laughed and played and ate so much,
Of the sweet and creamy fruit,
The Cheerful Chimpanzee was so happy,
He couldn't help but hoot.
The music played and the fire burned,
As the stars shone bright above,
They all danced and sang and cheered,
For the Cheerful Chimpanzee's Banana Party of love.
The night was young, and the fun was grand,
As they all enjoyed the fest,
The Cheerful Chimpanzee and his friends,
Were the happiest of all the rest.
So let us all take a lesson,
From the Cheerful Chimpanzee's Banana Party,
For when life gives us lemons,
We should make a sweet and delicious hearty.

The Talent Show Tiger's Big Performance

The Talent Show Tiger took the stage,
With nerves of steel and fierce intent,
He had practiced long and hard,
For this one moment, his big event.
The crowd was hushed, the spotlight bright,
As he began his show,
He sang and danced and played his guitar,
And wowed the audience, head to toe.
He sang of love and loss,
And the power of the wild,
He strummed his guitar with such finesse,
And had the crowd completely beguiled.
The Talent Show Tiger was a hit,
With his unique and special art,
He had the crowd on their feet,
Clapping and cheering, heart to heart.
So let us all take a lesson,
From the Talent Show Tiger's big performance,
For with hard work and dedication,
We too can shine with confidence.

Bouncing Bunnies

Bouncing Bunnies, hopping high,
Through fields of green and flowers bright,
With ears that flop and tails that wag,
They frolic in the morning light.
They nibble on the tender grass,
And chase each other round and round,
Their joyous play, a sight to see,
A symphony without a sound.
They dart and weave, and jump and spin,
With boundless energy and glee,
Bouncing Bunnies, so full of life,
A reminder to be wild and free.
But as the sun begins to set,
And shadows start to grow,
The Bouncing Bunnies take their rest,
And wait for tomorrow's show.
So let us all take a lesson,
From the Bouncing Bunnies' carefree play,
For life is short, and meant to be enjoyed,
In every single day.

Froggy Went a Hopping

Froggy went a hopping,
Through the lily pads and reeds,
He croaked a tune, so merrily,
As he fulfilled his needs.
He leapt from pond to pond,
With his long legs and webbed feet,
Exploring the world around him,
So full of wonder and sweet.
He caught a fly, with a quick snap,
And gobbled it down with glee,
Froggy went a hopping,
As happy as can be.
But as the day began to fade,
And the sun set in the west,
Froggy went back to his home,
And took a well-deserved rest.
So let us all take a lesson,
From Froggy's hopping and croaking,
For life is meant to be lived,
With joy and without joking.

Penguin Parade

The Penguin Parade, a sight to see,
Marching in a line so neat,
With their tuxedo-like coats,
And their waddling, shuffling feet.
They march in perfect synch,
Through the snow and ice so cold,
Their destination, unknown,
But their journey, brave and bold.
They huddle close, for warmth,
In the harsh and bitter weather,
Their determination, unbroken,
Their spirits, light as a feather.
They are a symbol of unity,
And the power of teamwork,
The Penguin Parade, a reminder,
Of the strength in numbers, it seems.
So let us all take a lesson,
From the Penguin Parade's march,
For together, we can accomplish,
Anything we set our hearts.

Monkey Business

Monkey Business, high in the trees,
Swinging from branch to branch with ease,
With their long tail and agile limbs,
They move with grace and playful whims.
They chatter and laugh, and play their games,
With fruits and nuts as their treasures,
Monkey Business, a joyful thing,
A daily routine of leisure.
They groom each other with care,
And share their food with their kin,
Monkeys, a symbol of family,
And the bonds that tie them within.
But sometimes they get into mischief,
Stealing and tricking with their wit,
Monkey Business, a reminder,
That balance is needed, bit by bit.
So let us all take a lesson,
From the monkeys in the trees,
For a little mischief is okay,
But balance is the key to life's breeze.

Turtle's Slow and Steady Race

Turtle's slow and steady pace,
Through the forest and across the space,
With determination in its eyes,
It moves forward without any guise.
Though others may pass it by,
With speed and agility,
Turtle knows it will arrive,
With persistence and reliability.
For slow and steady wins, the race,
In the end, it's true,
And turtle's hard work and grace,
Will see it through.
So let the hares and the rabbits run,
With all their might and haste,
For turtle's steady journey on,
Will lead to its rightful place.

Elephant's Trunkful of Tricks

Elephant's trunk, long and strong,
A trunkful of tricks all day long,
With its tip it can pluck a fruit,
And with its strength, it can move a root.
It can spray water on its back,
And with it, it can make a track,
It can trumpet loud and clear,
And show its joy and no fear.
It's a tool for drinking and eating,
For greeting and for trumpeting,
It's a symbol of power and might,
An elephant's trunk is a wondrous sight.
With its trunk, it can show its love,
And with it, it can show a shove,
It's a part of elephant's grace,
And it's a trunkful of tricks to embrace.

Kangaroo Jumps

Kangaroo jumps, high and far,
Through the outback, under the stars,
With its powerful legs, strong and true,
It bounces along, as if it's on cue.
With a thump and a bound,
It covers the ground,
And with each leap, it goes higher,
Showing off its amazing fire.
It's a sight to behold,
As it moves so bold,
With its joey in its pouch,
It's a mother and a vouch.
For the strength and the grace,
Of the kangaroo's pace,
As it jumps through the land,
It's a true wonder to stand.

Lion's Roar

Lion's roar echoes through the night,
A sound of power, fierce and bright,
It echoes through the savannah,
Making all who hear it tremble.
With a mane of gold and eyes of fire,
It commands the pride, its heart's desire,
It stalks its prey with stealth and grace,
A hunter, at the top of its race.
With a roar, it calls its pride,
To gather and to hunt, side by side,
With power and unity, they conquer all,
Their strength and bond, standing tall.
But the lion's roar is not just for show,
It's a call to arms, a call to know,
That the lion is the king of the land,
And its rule, forever to stand.
Through the trials and the fights,
The lion's roar guides with all its might,
It rallies the pride and gives them strength,
To defend their home, at any length.
For the lion's roar is not just a sound,
It's a symbol of power, profound,
It's the heartbeat of the savannah,
And the ruler of all that began.
So, when you hear the lion's roar,
Let it fill you with wonder and awe,
For it's the voice of the king,
And the anthem of the wild, it will sing.

Bear Necessities

In the dense woods of the forest,
Lives a creature big and robust,
With shaggy fur and sharp claws,
It roams the wild, without pause.
The bear, a symbol of strength and might,
With a roar that echoes through the night,
It forages for food, with tireless pace,
Living off the land, with grace.
With its keen sense of smell,
It can sniff out berries and nuts, as well,
With its powerful jaws, it can crack a shell,
And with its paws, it can dig a den, as well.
But the bear's life is not just about survival,
It's also about family and community's revival,
The mother bear raises her cubs with care,
Teaching them the ways of the wild, to share.
Bears are also known for their intelligence,
They are curious and have a sense of persistence,
They can learn to use tools and problem-solving,
They are more like us than we are involving.
But despite their strength and resilience,
Bears are facing many challenges, in existence,
Loss of habitat, hunting and human interference,
Are putting their future in an uncertain reference.
So let us remember the bear necessities,
Of respecting and preserving their abilities,
To live and thrive in the wild,
And ensure that their story doesn't go mild.

Panda-monium

In the lush bamboo forests of China,
Lives a creature, both sweet and serene,
With black and white fur, so soft and round,
It's a panda, the symbol of peace profound.
The panda, a creature so rare and unique,
With a diet that consists mainly of bamboo, it seeks,
It munches on the stalks, with contentment and glee,
A peaceful existence, as far as the eye can see.
But the panda's life is not all bamboo and rest,
They have to compete for resources and find a mate, at best,
Their populations are dwindling, due to habitat loss,
And human interference, at an alarming cost.
Conservation efforts are underway,
To protect the pandas and their habitat, every day,
Breeding programs and reforestation,
Are helping to boost their population.
But the pandas need more than just protection,
They need a holistic approach, for a sustainable connection,
To their habitat and the environment,
So they can thrive, without any lament.
So let us remember the panda-monium,
Of the importance of preserving their kingdom,
For the panda is not just a cute and cuddly bear,
But an important part of the ecosystem, to repair.

A Cat's Nine Lives

A cat, with fur soft as a cloud,
And eyes that gleam like jewels, proud,
With a tail that twitches and a purr that hums,
It's a creature that captivates, with its charm and whims.
A cat is known for its grace and agility,
With its sleek movements and silent agility,
It can jump and climb with ease,
And with its sharp claws, it can bring prey to its knees.
But a cat is also known for its independence,
It's a solitary creature, with a high tolerance,
It's a hunter, a survivor, and a protector,
And it can live a life, full of adventure.
The legend of a cat's nine lives,
Is a mystery that endures and thrives,
It's said that a cat has multiple lives,
And that it can come back, even after it dies.
But in reality, a cat's life is not infinite,
It's a precious gift, that should be treated with respect,
And it's our duty to care for them,
And to give them a life, full of love and freedom.
So let us remember a cat's nine lives,
As a symbol of resilience and survival,
And let us cherish and protect,
This graceful creature, that brings us so much respect.

Raccoon's Masked Banditry

In the dark of night, when all is still,
A creature roams the streets, with a bandit's thrill,
With its black mask and fluffy tail,
It's a raccoon, a creature with a tale.
Raccoons are known for their intelligence,
Their problem-solving skills and persistence,
They can open jars and cans with ease,
And raid trashcans, with great finesse.
But raccoons are also known for their curiosity,
They explore and learn, with great ferocity,
But this trait can also lead to danger,
When they come in contact with human strangers.
Raccoons are known for their banditry,
Stealing food and causing property,
But this is not out of malice,
But a natural instinct for survival and balance.
But with urbanization, raccoons' habitat is shrinking,
And their behavior is changing, and sometimes linking,
To diseases and conflicts with humans,
And it's important to find a solution that benefits.
So let us remember raccoon's masked banditry,
As a reminder of the importance of coexisting harmony,
By respecting their natural behaviors,
And finding a balance, that favors.

Piggy's Mud Bath

Piggy loved to roll in the mud,
With a smile on his face and a wag of his thud.
He'd squeal with delight as he wallowed and played,
Coating himself in a thick, brown glaze.
The sun beat down on the farm with its heat,
But Piggy didn't mind, he just found a muddy seat.
He'd splash and he'd snort and he'd have such fun,
Until the mud was his second skin, so warm and snug.
He'd make friends with the other pigs,
As they joined him in the mud, big wigs.
They'd play together and have a grand time,
Until it was time for them all to dine.
But Piggy's favorite part of the day,
Was when he'd lay in the mud and let it all sway.
He'd close his eyes and let out a sigh,
Content in the knowledge that he was living high.
The farmer would come and shake his head,
But Piggy knew he'd be back in the mud before bed.
For Piggy loved nothing more than his mud bath,
And nothing could ever take that away from his path.
So he'll roll and he'll play and he'll have his fun,
Coating himself in a thick, brown glaze,
And living his life just like a pig,
Happy and content in his mud bath gig.

Squirrel's Nutty Adventure

Squirrel scampered through the woods,
With a bushy tail and acorn goods.
He searched for nuts, both big and small,
To store for the winter, he'd gather them all.
He scampered up trees, with nimble feet,
Gathering walnuts, almonds, and sweet.
Chestnuts too, in a burr so tight,
He'd gnaw them open, with all his might.
He'd hide them away, in a hole in a tree,
To enjoy them later, in a cozy reverie.
But one day, as he gathered his hoard,
He heard a rustling, a strange discord.
He looked around, with eyes so bright,
And saw a fox, in the middle of the night.
He knew he had to act fast,
To protect his nuts, his winter repast.
He scampered and scurried, with all his might,
Leading the fox on a wild goose chase, in flight.
He zigged and zagged, through the trees,
Until the fox gave up, with a sigh of defeat on its knees.
Squirrel breathed a sigh of relief,
His nuts were safe, his worries were brief.
He gathered the last of his nutty treasure,
And scampered home, with great pleasure.
He munched on a nut, with a smile so wide,
Feeling victorious, on his nutty ride.
And as the winter came and went,
He knew his nutty adventure was well spent.
For the squirrel had proven his worth,
In his nutty adventure, he had saved his hoard,

And though the fox may try again,
The Squirrel knew he'd be ready, till the very end.

Fuzzy Wuzzy Caterpillar

Fuzzy Wuzzy Caterpillar, crawling on the ground
With your fluffy fur, you astound
Through the fields and gardens you roam
Making your way towards your ultimate home
With your many legs, you move with grace
Through the tall grass, at your own pace
Eating leaves as you go along
Growing bigger, you become strong
Months go by, and you've grown quite a bit
It's time to make a cocoon, you know it
But before you do, you'll eat one last meal
To fuel your transformation, what a big deal
Wrapped up tight, you'll stay for a while
But soon enough, you'll emerge with a smile
A beautiful butterfly, now you are
With wings that shimmer, you'll travel far
Fuzzy Wuzzy Caterpillar, you've come so far
From crawling on the ground, to reaching for the stars
You've shown us all, that change can be grand
And that beauty can be found in every stage of life's grand plan.

Silly Old Giraffe

Silly old Giraffe, with your long and slender neck
You tower above the others, with a sense of respect
With your spots and your lashes, you're quite a sight
You move with such grace, as you wander in the light
In the savannah you roam, with the sun on your face
Eating leaves from the trees, with your delicate grace
You're a gentle giant, with a heart full of love
And a spirit that soars, like a dove
You're a creature of wonder, with a unique design
From the tips of your toes, to the top of your spine
You're a living reminder, of the beauty of nature
And the power of creation, that's truly a capture
But despite your grandeur, you're also quite silly
You play and you frolic, like a child, so frilly
You stick out your tongue, and make silly faces
And make all the other animals, smile with their graces
Silly old Giraffe, you're a true treasure
With your kindness and joy, you bring pleasure
You remind us all, to take life with a grain of salt
And to never take ourselves, too seriously, after all.

Bouncing Baby Kangaroo

Bouncing Baby Kangaroo, with your tiny legs
You hop and you jump, with such energy and zest
With your fluffy ears, and your cute little nose
You're a bundle of joy, in your mother's pouch you doze
You are born so small, no bigger than a bean
But you grow quickly, and soon you'll be seen
Peeking out from your mother's pouch, with curious eyes
Watching the world, as you grow in size
You'll learn to hop and jump, with your strong back legs
You'll bound through the outback, with your playful pegs
And as you grow, you'll learn to survive
In the harsh Australian wilderness, you'll thrive
With your mother's guidance, and her loving care
You'll learn to find food, and to beware
Of the dangers that lurk, in the land down under
But with your strength and spirit, you'll overcome and wonder
Bouncing Baby Kangaroo, you're a true delight
With your bouncy energy, and your curious sight
You remind us all, of the beauty of youth
And the potential we all have, to grow and to sooth
You're a symbol of resilience, and the power of love
And a reminder to always keep bouncing, no matter what's above
You are a precious part of the wild, and a treasure of the earth
And we are lucky to have you, bouncing around since your birth.

Penguin Parade

Penguin Parade, marching in a line
Through the snow and ice, with a heart full of shine
With banners held high, and costumes so grand
We'll show the world, our home and our land
We'll waddle and hop, with our little legs
In perfect unison, our bodies we'll beg
To tell the story, of our home so true
And the beauty that surrounds us, for all to view
We'll glide on the ice, like a symphony
With a rhythm and grace, that's unique and free
We'll show the world, the wonder of our kind
And the joy that we find, in the land of our mind
We'll show them the love, that we share among
With the family and friends, that we hold so strong
We'll show them the strength, that we gain from the cold
And the resilience, that we've been told
We'll show them the beauty, that can be found
In the land of the ice, where the white and the sound
Mingle together, in a dance so true
To create a world, that's pure and new
Penguin Parade, we march with pride
To show the world, our home, and our guide
We hope you'll join us, in this march so true
To experience, the beauty of the Penguin Parade, that's new.

Wiggly Worms

Wiggly Worms, wriggling in the soil
Squirming and squirming, with your wriggling toil
With your slimy skin, and your segmented body
You are the unsung heroes, of the earth's ecology
You dig and you burrow, through the dirt and the clay
Aerating the soil, in a way that's astray
You break down the organic matter, and help it to blend
Into the earth, to help new life to tend
You are the recyclers, of the natural world
With your wiggling and wriggling, you help the earth unfurled
You break down the dead leaves, and turn them to humus
Giving back to the earth, a rich and abundant bonus
You are the food, for the birds and the beasts
A source of nutrition, for all the least
You are the foundation, for the web of life
And the key to the balance, of the natural strife
Wiggly Worms, though small and obscure
You play a vital role, in the earth's grand allure
You may be unseen, but your impact is grand
You are the silent workers, of the earth's great land
You are an essential part of the ecosystem,
And without you the soil would not be healthy.
You help plants to grow, and animals to thrive.
You are the unsung heroes, of the natural world.

Crazy Crocodile

Crazy Crocs, with your scaly skin
You lurk in the water, with a grin
With your powerful jaws, and your sharp teeth
You're a force to be reckoned with, underneath
You slide through the water, with a stealthy grace
With your eyes on the lookout, for your next chase
You're a predator, at the top of the food chain
A hunter and a killer, in the watery terrain
You're feared by many, and misunderstood
But there's more to you, than people think they should
You've been around for millions of years
A survivor, through all the changing spheres
You're a symbol of power, and endurance
A reminder, of the natural world's insurance
You're a part of the balance, in the ecosystem
And a vital link, in the circle of life's kingdom
But despite your fearsome reputation,
You have a playful side too.
You can be seen basking in the sun,
Or playing in the water with your family and friends.
Crazy Crocs, you are a true wonder
With your strength and your grace, you'll always be a thunder
You're a part of the natural world, that can't be ignored
A living relic, that has evolved and stored
You're a reminder of the past, and a hope for the future
A symbol of the wild, that will forever be a nurture.

Butterfly Boogie

Butterfly Boogie, fluttering in the breeze
With your colorful wings, you bring a sense of ease
You dance and you prance, in the warm sunshine
With your graceful moves, you bring joy to all in line
You fly from flower to flower, sipping nectar with glee
With your delicate antennae, you're a sight to see
You're a symbol of transformation, and new beginnings
A reminder that change can be beautiful, and worth winning
You start out as a caterpillar, crawling on the ground
But through metamorphosis, you are transformed, and truly astound
You emerge as a butterfly, with wings so bright
And take to the skies, with all your might
You fly freely, with the wind in your wings
With your boogying and bopping, you bring joy to everything
You're a reminder that beauty can be found, in the most unexpected
places
And that with a little faith, anything is possible and embraces
Butterfly Boogie, you bring color to the world
With your fluttering dance, you bring a sense of swirl
You remind us to let go of our fears, and to spread our wings
And to embrace the beauty, that life always brings.

Lazy Lion

Lazy Lion, lounging in the sun
With your mane so golden, and your roar second to none
You lay on the savannah, with a sense of ease
Watching the world go by, with a nonchalant breeze
You are the king of the jungle, with a regal air
But you prefer to spend your days, without a care
You nap and you lounge, with a sense of pride
And let the others, be the ones to provide
You let the lionesses, do the hunting and the work
While you rest and relax, like a true king's perk
But don't be fooled, by your lazy demeanor
You are a force to be reckoned with, a true believer
You are the protector, of your pride and your land
And when danger threatens, you take a stand
With your powerful roar, and your sharp claws
You defend your kingdom, with a sense of laws
Lazy Lion, you may seem indolent
But you are a true leader, with a sense of content
You remind us that rest and relaxation, is just as important as hard
work
And that balance, is key to living life with a sense of perk.

Dancing Dolphins

Dancing Dolphins, flipping and jumping in the sea
With your playful nature, you bring joy to all who see
You glide through the water, with a fluid grace
With your intelligence, you leave a lasting trace
You communicate, with a language all your own
A symphony of clicks and whistles, that's been known
To be a complex and intricate, form of speech
That's unique among animals, within their reach
You play and you frolic, with a sense of fun
With your acrobatic moves, you're second to none
You're a symbol of freedom, and of joy
A reminder to live life, with a sense of deploy
You are the guardians, of the ocean's health
With your presence, you bring a sense of wealth
You're a vital part of the ecosystem,
And a reminder of the beauty, that life can bring them
Dancing Dolphins, you're a true delight
With your playful nature, you bring a sense of light
You remind us to find joy, in the simple things
And to embrace the beauty, that life always brings.

Giggly Gorilla

Giggly Gorilla, with your fur so black
You sit in the jungle, with a sense of knack
For making others laugh, with your silly ways
You bring joy to the forest, with your playful plays
You swing from the vines, with a sense of glee
With your strong arms and hands, you're a sight to see
You eat your fill of leaves, and fruits too
Then you spend the rest of the day, doing what you do
You groom your family, with a tender touch
And play with the young ones, with a sense of such
You're a gentle giant, with a heart full of love
And a spirit that soars, like a white dove
But sometimes, you can't help but let out a giggle
When you're tickled or amused, you wiggle and waggle
Your contagious laughter, echoes through the trees
Bringing joy to all who hear, with a sense of ease
Giggly Gorilla, you're a true treasure
With your kindness and joy, you bring pleasure
You remind us all, to take life with a grain of salt
And to never take ourselves, too seriously, after all.

The Silly Monkey's Song

Silly Monkeys, swinging through the trees
With your playful nature, you bring joy and ease
You chatter and you hoot, with a sense of fun
With your silly antics, you're second to none
You swing from branch to branch, with a sense of grace
With your long arms and legs, you leave a lasting trace
You eat your fill of fruits and leaves, with a grin
Then you spend the rest of the day, doing monkey things
You play and you frolic, with a sense of glee
With your curious minds, you're always eager to see
What's going on around you, with a sense of wonder
You're a bundle of curiosity, that never goes under
But sometimes, you can't help but let out a giggle
When you're tickled or amused, you wiggle and waggle
Your contagious laughter, echoes through the trees
Bringing joy to all who hear, with a sense of ease
Silly Monkeys, you're a true delight
With your playful nature, you bring a sense of light
You remind us to find joy, in the simple things
And to embrace the beauty, that life always brings
So come along and join the fun, in the monkey's song
Sing and dance with them, all day long
Let your worries go, and let your spirit fly
With the silly monkeys, as they swing on by.

The Dancing Elephant

In the jungle, deep and dense,
Lived an elephant, immense.
With trunk held high, and ears outspread,
He danced and pranced, his heart full-fed.
He swayed his head to the rhythm of the drums,
As he moved his feet, like a river runs.
He dipped and swayed, to the beat of the song,
And the jungle cheered, as he danced along.
His trunk was his partner, as he dipped and twirled,
To the music that his heart unfurled.
With each step, the ground shook,
And the trees trembled, as if to look.
The monkeys chattered, and the birds sang,
As the elephant danced, his spirit rang.
He was the king of the jungle, wild and free,
Dancing to the beat of eternity.
As the sun set, and the stars shone,
The dancing elephant found his way home.
But in his dreams, he danced again,
In the jungle, where his spirit began.
And when the morning light shone through,
The elephant danced anew.
For in his heart, the music played,
And he danced, unafraid.
So let us all dance, like the elephant in the jungle,
With our hearts open, and our spirit's full bungle.
For life is but a dance, and we are all just players,
Let us make the most of it, and let our spirits be carriers.

The Singing Giraffe

The Singing Giraffe, tall and proud,
With spots all over, and a neck so bowed,
A creature of grace, in the savannah's space,
With a voice that echoes, in a melodic pace.
In the morning sun, she sings her song,
A tune so sweet, it never goes wrong,
The other animals, they gather round,
To hear her voice, a beautiful sound.
She sings of love, and she sings of hope,
Of the beauty of life, and how to cope,
With the struggles and hardships, we all must face,
She reminds us all, to find our place.
With a heart so pure, and a spirit so true,
The Singing Giraffe, is a sight to view,
She reminds us all, to be kind and strong,
To stand tall and sing our own song.
So let us all, learn from the giraffe,
To sing our hearts out, with a laugh,
For life is short, and time is fleeting,
But the memories of her singing, are always fleeting.
So let us all, be like the giraffe,
Sing our hearts out, with grace and laugh,
For in this world, full of chaos and pain,
The singing giraffe reminds us to sing again.

The Joking Crocodile

The Joking Crocodile, in the river he dwells,
With a grin on his face, and a laugh that tells,
Of a creature full of wit, and humor too,
Who always has a joke, to see you through.
He lounges in the sun, on the riverbank,
Telling tales and jokes, that will make you prance,
With laughter and glee, at his silly quips,
His humor so dry, it'll make your lips pucker and lips.
He tells jokes of the fish, who swim in the stream,
And the birds in the trees, who always seem to dream,
He tells of the monkeys, who swing in the trees,
And the lions who roar, with the greatest of ease.
But the Joking Crocodile's favorite joke by far,
Is the one about the turtle, who's always so slow,
He tells it with a grin, and a twinkle in his eye,
And the laughter that follows, can reach up to the sky.
But there's one thing you should know, about the Joking Crocodile,
He may seem all fun and games, but he's also quite vile,
For when the time is right, and his prey is in sight,
He'll snap and he'll bite, with all his might.
So, beware of the Joking Crocodile,
With his wit and his jokes, and his crocodile smile,
For while he may make you laugh, and forget your woes,
He's also a predator, who knows how to dispose.
So let us all, learn from the Joking Crocodile,
To enjoy the little things, and laugh with a smile,
For in this world, full of stress and strife,
A good joke can bring a little more light to our life.

The Whistling Whale

The Whistling Whale, in the ocean deep,
With a song so sweet, it's like a lullaby to sleep,
A creature of grace, in the vast blue sea,
With a voice that echoes, so melodically.
In the midnight moon, she sings her tune,
A melody so pure, it's like a symphony in June,
The other creatures, they listen in awe,
To hear her voice, a symphony raw.
She sings of love, and she sings of hope,
Of the beauty of life, and how to cope,
With the struggles and hardships, we all must face,
She reminds us all, to find our place.
With a heart so big, and a spirit so true,
The Whistling Whale, is a sight to view,
She reminds us all, to be kind and strong,
To stand tall and sing our own song.
So let us all, learn from the whale,
To sing our hearts out, with a tale,
For life is short, and time is fleeting,
But the memories of her singing, are always fleeting.
So let us all, be like the whale,
Sing our hearts out, with a tale,
For in this world, full of chaos and pain,
The Whistling Whale reminds us to sing again.
She sings of the ocean's depth,
Of the creatures that call it home,
She sings of the storms that rage,
And the calm that follows.
With each note she sings,
She tells the story of the sea,

Of its beauty and its mysteries,
Of its secrets yet to be revealed.
She sings of the whales that came before,
And the ones that will come after,
Of the circle of life and death,
And the eternal dance of the ocean.
So let us all, listen to the Whistling Whale,
With open hearts and open ears,
For in her song, we will find,
The wisdom of the sea, and all its years.

The Hula Hooping Hippo

The Hula Hooping Hippo, in the river she dips,
With a hoop on her hip, and a smile on her lips,
A creature of grace, in the water she flows,
With a rhythm so smooth, it glows.
In the afternoon sun, she spins her hoop,
A dance so lively, it's like a firework loop,
The other animals, they gather round,
To watch her hoop, with a joyful sound.
She spins to the beat, of the river's flow,
And the laughter of the birds, as they fly low,
She spins with the grace, of a swan in flight,
And the rhythm of the drums, that ignite.
With a heart full of joy, and a spirit full of play,
The Hula Hooping Hippo, is a sight to see today,
She reminds us all, to have fun and be free,
To dance to the beat, of our own destiny.
So let us all, learn from the hippo,
To hula hoop with joy, and let our spirits glow,
For life is short, and time is fleeting,
But the memories of her hula hooping, are always fleeting.
So let us all, be like the hippo,
Hula hoop with joy, and let our spirits flow,
For in this world, full of chaos and pain,
The Hula Hooping Hippo reminds us to let go and play again.
She spins with the water, as it flows and flows,
And the fish that swim, as they come and go,
She spins with the breeze, as it blows and blows,
And the flowers that bloom, as they grow and grow.
She spins with the sun, as it shines and shines,
And the shadows that fall, as the day declines,

She spins with the moon, as it rises and sets,
And the stars that twinkle, as the night forgets.
So let us all, follow the Hula Hooping Hippo,
In her dance, we will find,
The rhythm of life, and the beat of our hearts,
And the joy that never departs.

The Juggling Jaguar

The Juggling Jaguar, in the jungle he roams,
With balls in his paws, and a smile on his dome,
A creature of agility, in the wilds he moves,
With a grace that proves, he's got the skills to groove.
In the early morning light, he juggles with ease,
A performance so smooth, it's like a gentle breeze,
The other animals, they gather round,
To watch him juggle, with a smile profound.
He juggles with fire, and he juggles with knives,
And the other animals, they marvel at his life,
He juggles with fruit, and he juggles with balls,
And the other animals, they cheer, as he enthralls.
With a heart full of passion, and a spirit full of fun,
The Juggling Jaguar, is a sight to see, under the sun,
He reminds us all, to chase our dreams,
To juggle our responsibilities and make them gleam.
So let us all, learn from the Jaguar,
To juggle with passion, and let our spirits soar,
For life is short, and time is fleeting,
But the memories of his juggling, are always fleeting.
So let us all, be like the Jaguar,
Juggle with passion, and let our spirits soar,
For in this world, full of chaos and pain,
The Juggling Jaguar reminds us to never give up and to keep the flame.
He juggles with the leaves, as they fall and fall,
And the wind that blows, as it calls and calls,
He juggles with the rain, as it pours and pours,
And the thunder that roars, as it scores and scores.
He juggles with the stars, as they twinkle and shine,
And the moon that rises, as it aligns and aligns,

He juggles with the fireflies, as they flicker and flash,
And the night that falls, as it crashes and crashes.
So let us all, follow the Juggling Jaguar,
In his performance, we will find,
The rhythm of life, and the grace of our souls,
And the passion that never grows old.

The Tickling Toucan

Deep in the heart of the jungle,
Where the vines are thick and the trees are tall,
Lives a bird of vibrant colors,
A toucan, with a beak so bright and tall.
With feathers black as the night sky,
And yellow hues that shine like gold,
He dances through the canopy,
His movements bold and bold.
His laughter echoes through the land,
A symphony of joy and mirth,
As he flits and flutters, so grand,
A creature of great worth.
His beak is a thing of wonder,
Long and curved with a rainbow sheen,
The perfect tool for plucking fruit,
And tickling the noses of those, so keen.
But the toucan's tickling is not all fun,
For it serves a purpose, under the sun.
With a gentle touch, he'll tickle a friend,
To show affection, till the very end.
So, if you're ever in the jungle green,
And you hear a laugh, so serene,
Keep an eye out, for the tickling toucan,
A true friend, in a world of fauna.
With his wings outspread, he soars so high,
A sight to behold, in the morning sky,
His beauty shines like a beacon bright,
A reminder of the wonders of nature's might.
Through the lush and verdant jungle,
The tickling toucan takes flight,

A symbol of joy and laughter,
A beacon of hope, shining bright.
So let us all take a cue from the toucan,
And spread love, kindness, and cheer,
For in this world, filled with beauty,
We all have a purpose here.

The Rapping Rhinoceros

Deep in the savannah, where the grass is tall,
Lives a creature fierce and strong,
With a horn upon his snout,
And a beat that can't be wrong.
The rapping rhinoceros, with skin so tough,
Marching to the rhythm of his own drums,
His voice booms loud and clear,
A sound that never hums.
With every step he takes,
The earth beneath him shakes,
His rhymes flow like a river,
His flow never breaks.
He's got a style all his own,
A flow that's smooth and tight,
His rhymes are sharp and clever,
A true lyrical delight.
He's a master of the mic,
A rapper without peer,
His rhymes are always fresh,
A sound that's always dear.
With every verse he drops,
The crowd goes wild with glee,
For the rapping rhinoceros,
Is a true lyrical king, you'll see.
He's got a heart of gold,
And a spirit that's free,
His rhymes are a reflection,
Of the soul that's wild and free.
He's a force to be reckoned with,
A rapper that's here to stay,

With his horn held high,
He'll lead the way.
So, when you're out in the savannah,
And you hear a beat that's hot,
Just know that the rapping rhinoceros,
Is tearing up the spot.
With his powerful rhymes,
And his fierce flow,
He'll leave you mesmerized,
And wanting more, you'll know.
So, let's all give it up,
For the rapping rhinoceros,
A true expert in the mic,
A rapper that's truly boss.
He'll take us on a journey,
Through the savannah's wild,
With his rhymes as our guide,
We'll dance and sing like a child.
So come on, let's all join in,
And rap along with the rhinoceros,
For in this world of wonder,
There's no limit to what we can accomplish.

The Kicking Kangaroo

In the land down under, where the eucalyptus stands,
Lives a creature fierce and strong, with powerful legs and hands.
The kicking kangaroo, with a bound so swift and true,
Leaps across the outback, with a kick that's fierce and new.
With fur as red as the desert sands,
And a tail as long as the great barrier reef,
He's a symbol of the wild and free,
A creature that's truly unique.
His legs are strong and powerful,
A force to be reckoned with,
With every kick he makes,
The earth beneath him shakes.
But it's not just his strength,
That sets the kangaroo apart,
It's his fierce determination,
That beats within his heart.
For in the face of adversity,
He never backs down,
He stands tall and proud,
With his head held high and his feet on the ground.
He's a true warrior of the wild,
A champion of the outback,
With his kicks and his hops,
He'll never be held back.
So, when you're wandering the outback,
And you hear a sound so loud,
Just know that the kicking kangaroo,
Is tearing up the crowd.
With his powerful legs,
And his fierce determination,

He'll leave you in awe,
Of his true kangaroo sensation.
So, let's all give it up,
For the kicking kangaroo,
A true warrior of the wild,
A creature that's truly true blue.
For in this world of wonder,
There's no limit to what we can achieve,
With a kick and a hop,
We too can soar and believe.
So come on, let's all join in,
And kick along with the kangaroo,
For in this world of beauty,
There's a place for me and you.

Bouncing Bunnies, Hopping Along

In the meadow, where the wildflowers grow,
Lives a creature soft and small,
With long ears that flop and fluffy tails,
They're the bouncing bunnies, hopping along.
With fur as white as the falling snow,
And eyes that shine like the morning sun,
They hop and play in the fields,
Their energy never done.
Their long legs are strong and agile,
Built for jumping and bounding,
With every hop they make,
Their spirits are resounding.
They're a symbol of new beginnings,
And the joys of spring,
With their playful antics,
Their hearts take wing.
But it's not just their playfulness,
That sets the bunnies apart,
It's their gentle nature,
That warms the heart.
For in the face of danger,
They'll run and hide,
But in peaceful moments,
They'll come out to glide.
They're a true wonder of nature,
A delight to see,
With their soft and fluffy fur,
And their hopping energy.
So, when you're wandering the meadow,
And you hear a sound so light,

Just know that the bouncing bunnies,
Are hopping out of sight.
With their soft and cuddly appearance,
And their gentle disposition,
They'll leave you feeling enchanted,
With their adorable disposition.
So, let's all give it up,
For the bouncing bunnies,
A true wonder of nature,
A delight to see.
For in this world of beauty,
There's a place for all to thrive,
With a hop and a skip,
We too can come alive.
So come on, let's all join in,
And hop along with the bunnies,
For in this world of wonder,
There's a place for all to be happy.

Wriggling Worms, Burrowing Deep

In the soil, where the earth is rich and dark,
Lives a creature small and humble,
With wriggling bodies and no legs,
They're the wriggling worms, burrowing deep.
With skin as brown as the autumn leaves,
And a texture that's smooth and slick,
They tunnel through the earth,
Their movement quick.
Their wriggling bodies are strong,
Built for digging and burrowing,
With every inch they move,
Their contributions are astounding.
They're a symbol of hard work and dedication,
And the importance of the unseen,
With their tireless labor,
The earth becomes a green.
But it's not just their strength,
That sets the worms apart,
It's their role in the ecosystem,
That plays a vital part.
For they're the ones that help to aerate the soil,
And enrich it with their waste,
Allowing plants to grow,
And the cycle to take place.
They're a true wonder of nature,
A creature often overlooked,
But without them,
The balance would be shook.
So, when you're wandering the garden,
And you see a worm at play,

Just know that the wriggling worm,
Is working hard today.
With their small and unassuming appearance,
And their quiet disposition,
They're performing a vital role,
In the health of our ecosystems and oceans.
So, let's all give it up,
For the wriggling worms,
A true wonder of nature,
A creature that's worth to learn.
For in this world of beauty,
There's a place for all to thrive,
With their wriggling and burrowing,
They keep the earth alive.
So come on, let's all take notice,
And appreciate the wriggling worms,
For in this world of wonder,
They're playing an important term.

Froggy Fun

In the pond, where the lily pads float,
Lives a creature slimy and green,
With webbed feet and a croak so deep,
They're the froggy friends, so serene.
With skin as smooth as the rippling water,
And a color that blends with the leaves,
They swim and play in the pond,
Their happiness never leaves.
Their webbed feet are made for swimming,
Built for jumping and splashing,
With every leap they make,
Their fun is never-ending.
They're a symbol of playfulness and joy,
And the beauty of the natural world,
With their croaks and songs,
Their spirits are unfurled.
But it's not just their playfulness,
That sets the frogs apart,
It's their role in the ecosystem,
That plays a vital part.
For they're the ones that help control the insect population,
And serve as an indicator of the health of the environment,
Their presence is crucial,
For the balance of nature to be bent.
They're a true wonder of nature,
A creature often underappreciated,
But without them,
The ecosystem would be devastated.
So, when you're wandering by the pond,
And you hear a croak so loud,

Just know that the froggy friends,
Are singing their song proud.
With their slimy and green appearance,
And their playful disposition,
They're performing an important role,
In maintaining the health of the ecosystem and the oceans.
So, let's all give it up,
For the froggy friends,
A true wonder of nature,
A creature that's worth to befriend.
For in this world of beauty,
There's a place for all to thrive,
With their croaks and songs,
They help keep the balance alive.
So come on, let's all take notice,
And appreciate the froggy friends,
For in this world of wonder,
Their role is important to the end.

Otterly Amazing

Otterly amazing, the otter's grace
As it glides through the water with ease
Its furry body and playful face
A sight that is sure to please
With webbed paws for swimming so fast
And dense fur to keep warm
The otter's life is truly a blast
In rivers and oceans, it's the norm
They play and frolic all day long
With their family and friends
Their bonds are strong and true
Their love never ends
Their intelligence is quite impressive
Their tool use is quite rare
They crack open shellfish with a rock
And show their skills without a care
But otters are not just for fun
They play a vital role
In the ecosystem, they are one
Their presence helps keep the balance whole
So, let's protect and preserve
The otters in our seas
For they are otterly amazing
And a treasure for all to see.

Raccoon Rascals

Raccoon Rascals, mischievous and sly
With their bandit masks and bushy tails high
They roam the streets at night
In search of food, they take flight
With their nimble paws and sharp claws
They easily scale walls and gnaw
Through trash cans and gardens
Their foraging skills are quite harden
But don't let their antics fool you
These creatures are quite shrewd
They are survivors, through and through
In the wild, they always renew
Their intelligence is quite remarkable
They can solve problems with ease
Their memories are quite retentive
They remember where food can be gleaned with ease
But as we encroach on their natural habitat
Their lives are becoming harder
We must learn to coexist with these raccoon rascals
And work towards a more harmonious order
So, let's respect their wildness
And give them space to thrive
For these raccoon rascals
Are a vital part of life.
With their nightly adventures,
They keep us entertained,
Their antics and mischief,
Are truly unrefrained.
Raccoon Rascals,
They are creatures of the night,

With their bandit masks,
They are a true delight.
Through the alleys, they roam,
With their bushy tails, they hold,
Their secrets, their mysteries,
That are yet to be told.
But we must remember,
They are wild creatures,
And they deserve,
Their own natural features.
So let us protect,
And preserve their kind,
For these Raccoon Rascals,
Are truly one of a kind.
With their playful personalities,
And their cunning ways,
They remind us to live in the moment,
And to not take life too seriously, always.
So next time you see them,
Rummaging through your trash,
Remember these Raccoon Rascals,
And the important role they play, in the vast.

The Beaver's Great Work

With determination in his heart,
The beaver set out to start
Building his home on the river's edge,
A dam to protect and pledge
He works tirelessly, day and night
Chopping down trees with all his might
Dragging the logs to the river's flow
To create a dam, strong and aglow
The water rushes against the dam
But the beaver perseveres, he gives a damn
He mounds the mud, and stacks the sticks
His hard work, never ending tricks
As the dam grows taller and wider
Fish and wildlife, begin to reside
A new ecosystem is born
Thanks to the beaver's tireless morn
But the beaver's work is never done
For he must constantly maintain
The dam, to keep it strong
And the river from going astray
He tirelessly rebuilds and repairs
Through the seasons, without any scares
A true Master of Engineering
His dam, a true masterpiece, worth seeing
But the beaver's labor is not in vain
For his dam, brings life to the plain
A home for his family, and a haven for all
A reminder of the power of hard work and gall
So let us admire the beaver's toil
And the fruits of his labor, so royal

For he teaches us the value of hard work
And the beauty that can come from the dirt.

The Fox's Clever Hunt

With a sly grin and a wily glance,
The fox set out to take his chance
In the fields and the forest glade,
He'd hunt for his dinner, unafraid
He crept through the underbrush,
Silent as a mouse, not making a hush
His keen ears pricked, his nose to the ground,
Searching for the scent of his next round
He spots a rabbit, nibbling on grass,
And with a sudden dash, he's upon its ass
But the rabbit is quick, and darts away,
Leaving the fox to chase, without delay
But the fox is clever, and knows just how,
To outsmart his prey, and make them bow
He feigns to the left, then to the right,
And the rabbit falls for it, without a fight
The fox pounces, and makes the kill,
With a swift bite, the rabbit's fate is sealed still
But his work is not done, he must be sly,
For there may be danger lurking nearby
With his prize in tow, he disappears,
Into the night, without any fears
For he is an expert in his craft,
A clever fox, who'll outwit them all, at last.
He's a hunter of the night,
With his cleverness, he'll always come out right,
With his wits and his cunning,
He'll always have a full belly, nothing less.
His fur, as red as a flame,
Shining in the moonlight, his fame,

Will be known, for miles around,
A clever fox, without a sound.
But we must remember,
As we admire his skills,
That he is a wild animal,
And his actions are nature's wills.
So let us respect,
And coexist with him,
For this clever fox,
Is a part of nature's hymn.

The Goose's Silly Stride

With a honk and a waddle,
The goose set out to prattle
Along the pond, with a silly strut,
Making all the other birds cut
With his head held high in the air,
He honks and quacks without a care
His waddle is comical to see,
As he waddles along, so carefree
He dips his head in the water,
And splashes about, like a daughter
He paddles and preens, with a goofy grin,
Making the other birds grin
But the goose is not just silly,
He's also a bird of great willy,
He flies in formation, with his flock,
Migrating thousands of miles, without a knock
So, let's not judge the silly goose,
For his antics, we shouldn't muse,
For he's more than just a waddling clown,
He's a bird of great strength and renown.
With his silly honking,
And his waddling walk,
He brings joy and laughter,
To everyone who talks.
He's a bird of the sky,
And of the pond,
With his silly ways,
He'll always bond.
So let us enjoy,
The goose's antics,

For in this silly bird,
There's much to be manic.

Guardian Angel in Fur

There once was a loyal dog named Max,
Whose love for his family was simply a fact.
He'd wag his tail with glee,
Whenever they'd come to see,
And he'd follow them everywhere, in fact.
He'd bark at any stranger who came near,
Protecting his loved ones, with no fear.
He'd guard them day and night,
Making sure everything was right,
And he'd never leave their side, that's dear.
Max was more than just a pet,
He was a member of the family, you'd bet.
He'd comfort them in times of strife,
And bring them joy and love in life.
He was always there, that's no sweat.
Through sickness and health, he was there,
Through happiness and sorrow, he'd care.
He'd lay by their feet,
And make their worries retreat,
For Max was a loyal dog, beyond compare.
He may have been just a dog, you see,
But to his family, he was their key.
To a life filled with love and light,
For as long as Max was in sight,
They knew they'd always be safe and free.
So, here's to Max, the loyal and true,
Who gave his love, through and through.
A protector and friend, till the end,
For in our hearts, he'll always be new.

The Cuddly Bear with a Wild Heart

In the frozen tundra, white as snow,
Lived a cuddly and fluffy polar bear, oh so.
With fur as soft as cotton,
And a playful demeanor, he was quite the tonic.
He'd frolic in the ice and snow,
With grace and agility, he'd flow.
He'd chase the fish in the arctic sea,
And catch them with great glee.
His fur was a cloak of warmth,
Against the bitter, icy storm.
He'd curl up in a ball,
And take a nap, after a playful squall.
But don't let his cuddly exterior fool,
For he was a fierce hunter, fiercely cool.
He'd roam the land, with strength and might,
And claim his place, as the arctic's knight.
But when the day was done,
He'd cuddle up with his loved ones.
He'd let out a contented sigh,
And close his eyes, as the northern lights fly.
In the frozen wilderness, he roamed,
But in his heart, a love he had honed.
For the ice and snow, and all of his kin,
And the cuddly and fluffy polar bear, would always be grin.
So, here's to the cuddly and fluffy bear,
Who lives in the arctic, with love to spare.
May his fluffy fur always keep him warm,
And his playful spirit, forever charm.

The Lively Parrot of the Tropics

In the lush tropical trees,
A colorful and lively parrot, with grace and ease,
He'd flit and flutter, with a squawk and a screech,
Filling the forest with his vibrant speech.
With feathers as bright as a rainbow,
He'd soar and dip, like a graceful show.
He'd mimic the songs of the other birds,
And with his chatter, fill the forest with words.
He'd perch on a branch, with a tilt of his head,
Observing the world, with curiosity unled.
His beady eyes, shining with wonder and mirth,
As he took in the sights, of the tropical earth.
But when the day was done,
He'd return to his mate, with a playful run.
They'd cuddle close, in their nest,
And whisper sweet nothings, as they lay to rest.
So, here's to the colorful and lively parrot,
With his plumage, so bright and so awort.
May his vibrant spirit, never dim,
And his song, forever fill the jungle's rim.

The Snail's Unstoppable Climb

In the garden, under the leaves,
A determined and persistent snail, with will to achieve,
He'd inch his way, with a slow and steady pace,
Leaving a trail of slime, all over the place.
With his spiral shell, on his back,
He'd set his sights, on a new track.
He'd climb the stems, and scale the walls,
And never give up, through any falls.
He'd navigate through the thorns and the dirt,
With a determination, that wouldn't hurt.
He'd reach the top of the flower,
And take in the view, for hours.
But when the day was done,
He'd retreat to his shell, one by one.
He'd rest and rejuvenate,
For the next day's journey, to await.
So, here's to the determined and persistent snail,
With his slow and steady, never to fail.
May his willpower never dim,
And his determination, forever brim.
Though he might not be the fastest on the land,
His persistence and willpower will make him stand.
He will reach his goals, no matter how tall,
For determination is the key, for the snail, to stand tall.

The Swan's Graceful Swim

In a peaceful lake, surrounded by trees,
A graceful and elegant swan was so easy to please.
With a long neck, slender and white,
She swam through the water, with all her might.
Her feathers, soft as a fluffy cloud,
Rippled in the water, as she paddled around.
She'd dip her head, to catch a fish,
And with a graceful grace, she'd make a wish.
She'd float on the surface, with poise and style,
An embodiment of beauty, all the while.
Her reflection, mirrored on the calm lake's face,
A peaceful beauty, in this tranquil place.
But when the day was done,
She'd return to her mate, with a graceful run.
They'd nuzzle close, in their nest,
As the sun set in the west.
So, here's to the graceful and elegant swan,
With her beauty, that never wan.
May her grace, forever be,
And her elegance, for all to see.
A swan in the lake, a sight so grand,
A graceful bird, that walks on land.
With a long neck, and feathers so white,
She's a beauty, that will delight.
So next time you see a swan, so fair,
Take a moment to stop and stare.
For her grace and elegance, will take your breath away,
And make your heart sing, hooray!

The Firefly's Friendly Flicker

In the darkness, of the night,
A friendly and helpful firefly took flight.
With his glowing light, so bright,
He illuminated the darkness, with all his might.
He'd flit and flutter, through the trees,
Guiding the way, for all who please.
He'd light up the path, for those who stray,
And show them the way, without delay.
He'd dance and play, in the warm summer breeze,
With his light, a beacon of ease.
He'd light up the night, with a cheerful glow,
And help the lost, to find their way, they know.
But when the day was done,
He'd rest, till the next day begun.
He'd recharge his light, for the next night's journey,
And be ready to help, in a friendly manner, surely.
So, here's to the friendly and helpful firefly,
With his light, that never die.
May his helpfulness, never cease,
And his light, forever bring peace.

The Shy Deer's Song

In the forest, deep and wide,
A timid and shy deer would often hide.
With big brown eyes, so gentle and pure,
She'd watch the world, from her safe and secure.
She'd graze on the grass, with a gentle pace,
And avoid the loud, with a timid grace.
She'd jump at the sound, of a twig breaking,
And flee, at the sight of a human shaking.
She'd keep to herself, and stay away,
From the hustle and bustle, of the day.
But when the night was calm, and the moon was high,
She'd come out to play and let her spirit fly.
But when the day was done,
She'd retreat to her bed, and rest, one by one.
She'd dream of the day, when she can be free,
To be herself, and let her true self, be.
So, here's to the timid and shy deer,
With her gentle spirit, that's so sincere.
May she find the courage, to be who she is,
And let her light shine, without any fuss.

The Unstoppable Pup

In a cozy home, filled with love and cheer,
A playful and energetic puppy would often appear.
With wagging tail, and boundless energy,
He'd chase and fetch, with great agility.
He'd bark and yip, with a joyful tone,
And make the whole house, feel like home.
He'd jump and spin, with a wag of his tail,
And bring smiles to all, without fail.
He'd play with his toys, till he was tired,
And then lay on his bed and be admired.
He'd lick your face, with a slurp and a kiss,
And make your heart, feel like it's in bliss.
He'd follow you around, with a hop and a skip,
And be your constant companion, on your trip.
He'd be your loyal friend, through thick and thin,
And make your life, more fun and grin.
But when the day was done,
He'd lay by your feet, and rest, one by one.
He'd dream of tomorrow's adventure,
And be ready for it, with a wag of his tail, sure.
So, here's to the playful and energetic puppy,
With his boundless energy, that never run out, giddy.
May his playful spirit, never fade,
And his tail wag, forever be made.
Through his eyes, the world is a playground,
And every day, a new adventure awaits to be found.
With his boundless energy, and his joyful bark,
He brings joy to all and leaves a playful mark.

The Parakeet's Melodic Chatter

In a brightly colored cage, with a bell,
A noisy and chatty parakeet would often dwell.
With feathers as vibrant as a rainbow,
He'd sing and squawk, with a joyful flow.
He'd mimic the sounds, of the world around,
And make the house, with his chatter, resound.
He'd repeat the words, that you say,
And make you laugh, in a playful way.
He'd preen his feathers, with a tilt of his head,
And show off his colors, with a dance and a spread.
He'd swing on his perch, with a chirp and a tweet,
And make the whole house, feel so sweet.
But when the day was done,
He'd settle down, and rest, one by one.
He'd dream of tomorrow's chatter and sing,
And be ready for it, with a cheerful wing.
So, here's to the noisy and chatty parakeet,
With his vibrant colors, and a voice, so sweet.
May his chatter, never cease,
And his singing, forever bring peace.
Though he might be noisy, and make some noise,
His chatter is a joyful melody, that

The Ant's tireless Journey

In the bustling colony, deep underground,
A hardworking and dedicated ant could often be found.
With determination in her eyes, and strength in her mandibles,
She'd carry her load, with tireless labors.
She'd gather food, and build the nest,
With a tireless spirit, that never would rest.
She'd work all day, and all night long,

To keep the colony, thriving and strong.
She'd march in a line, with her sisters, in a chain,
To bring back the loot, from the food they'd gained.
She'd work without rest, without a break,
For the colony, her dedication, would never shake.
She'd tend to the young, and care for the old,
And keep the colony, safe from the cold.
She'd defend the colony, with her life,
For her duty, was to her colony, her duty as a wife.
But when the day was done,
She'd rest, with her sisters, one by one.
She'd dream of tomorrow's work,
And be ready for it, with a heart, that would never shirk.
So, here's to the hardworking and dedicated ant,
With her tireless spirit, and her strength, so grand.
May her work ethic, never falter,
And her colony, forever prosper.
Though small in size, and often overlooked,
The ant's dedication is a story, that should be told.
For they work tirelessly, day and night,
To build a colony, that's strong and bright.
With their teamwork and unity, they achieve,
what seems impossible for them to achieve,
Their hard work and dedication, a true testament,
to their strength and resilience, that's truly best.

The Peacock's Melodic Cry

In a lush garden, surrounded by blooms,
A colorful and vibrant peacock would often assume.
With feathers as bright as the rainbow,
He'd spread his tail, in a grand show.
He'd strut and preen, with a regal stance,
And show off his plumage, with a graceful dance.
He'd flash his tail, with a fan and a flourish,
And leave all in awe, with his grandeur.
He'd call out with a loud cry,
And fill the garden, with his melodic sigh.
He'd feast on the fruit, from the trees,
And enjoy the beauty, with the gentle breeze.
He'd watch over his peahens, with a watchful eye,
And protect them, from any harm, nearby.
He'd be the king, of the garden, with his grand display,
And leave all in wonder, with his beauty, in every way.
But when the day was done,
He'd retire to his roost, one by one.
He'd rest and rejuvenate,
For the next day's display, to await.
So, here's to the colorful and vibrant peacock,
With his grandeur, that's never out of stock.
May his beauty, forever be,
And his display, for all to see.
With his feathers as bright as the sun,
And his tail, that's second to none.
He walks with pride, and holds his head high,
A true regal beauty, in the sky.
His feathers, a rainbow of hues,
Each one a work of art, that can be viewed.

He is a symphony, of color and sound,
That leaves all in awe and leaves the ground.
His call, a melody, that echoes through the land,
Filled with beauty, and a touch of grand.
So next time you see a peacock, so fair,
Take a moment

A Hamster's Taco Odyssey

The hamster scurries through the fields,
A love for tacos in his heart,
He searches high and low,
For ingredients that will make the perfect start.
He grinds the corn, and shapes the dough,
Fries them up till they are hot,
And adds his fillings with care,
Till his tacos are a tasty lot.
He loves them spicy, with jalapenos,
Topped with sour cream and cheese,
He eats them morning, noon, and night,
His love for tacos will never cease.
He throws taco parties with his friends,
They dance and sing and make amends,
And even shares his tacos with those in need,
A taco loving hamster, a true friend indeed.
But one day, a tragedy strikes,
The taco stand shuts down,
The hamster's heart is broken,
His frown can be seen all around.
But he doesn't give up hope,
He searches far and wide,
And finds a new taco spot,
His love for tacos will never subside.
So, if you ever come across a taco loving hamster,
Don't be surprised, it's just his nature,
Just share a taco with him, and you'll see,
A friendship with a taco lover, forever to be.
His love for tacos is unending,
A passion that burns bright,

For the taco loving hamster,
Tacos will be his delight.
Through all of life's ups and downs,
His love for tacos will never wane,
For the taco loving hamster,
Tacos will forever remain.

The Fierce and Brave Wolf

Through the forest deep and dark,
A wolf roams with fierce and brave heart,
His howl echoes in the night,
A symbol of his wild and untamed might.
With piercing eyes and sharpened teeth,
He rules the land, the king of beasts,
His strength and power, unmatched,
A force to be reckoned with, unmatched.
He hunts with precision and skill,
His prey, no match for his will,
And when the moon is high and bright,
He howls with all his might.
But he's not just a hunter, fierce and strong,
He's a protector, of his pack, all along,
He'll defend his loved ones, till the end,
A true leader, a true friend.
Through blizzards and storms, he'll lead the way,
Guiding his pack, come what may,
And when the danger has passed,
He'll lay down and rest at last.
He's a symbol of freedom and wildness,
A creature of beauty and finesse,
And though some may fear his might,
He's a fierce and brave wolf, a true sight.

The Strong and Mighty Gorilla

In the jungle deep and green,
A gorilla stands, strong and serene,
His muscles rippling with power,
A symbol of his might every hour.
With a chest as broad as a barrel,
And arms as thick as a tree trunk,
He commands respect from all,
A ruler of the jungle, never to be outdone.
He roams the land with grace and ease,
His presence, a force that can't be appeased,
He forages for food, and builds his nest,
A king among gorillas, truly the best.
But he's not just a brute with strength,
He's a thinker, with a mind of great length,
He uses tools, and shows empathy,
A being of intelligence, a true rarity.
He'll fiercely protect his family and troop,
From any threat, he'll never stoop,
And when the young ones play and swing,
He'll watch over them, his heart taking wing.
He's a symbol of strength and intelligence,
A creature of beauty and resilience,
And though some may fear his power,
He's a strong and mighty gorilla, every hour.
Through the trials of life, he'll stand tall,
A leader and protector, to one and all,
And when his time on earth is through,
His legacy will live on, forever true.

The Tiger's Friendship

In the jungle, wild and fun,
Lives a tiger, majestic and regal, everyone
With stripes so bright, orange, and black,
He's the king of the jungle, that's a fact.
He roams the land with grace and pride,
With a roar so loud, it echoes far and wide,
He's strong and fierce, yet kind and true,
A friend to all, he'll protect and guide you.
He loves to play, and chase his tail,
And when he's tired, he'll take a nap, without fail,
But when it's time to hunt for food,
He'll use his stealth and skills, that are so good.
He's a protector of his family and his home,
And will defend them, till the end, he'll never roam,
And when the young ones play and swing,
He'll watch over them, his heart taking wing.
He's a symbol of strength and courage,
And even though he's big and fierce,
He's also gentle, kind and wise,
And will always be a friend, that will never tire.
So, if you ever come across a tiger,
In the wild and fun jungle,
Don't be afraid, he'll be your guide,
And together, you'll have a great bundle.
He's the king of the jungle,
A majestic and regal tiger,
A true friend, who will always be there,
To protect and guide you, with care.

The Cuddly Koala

In the eucalyptus trees, up high,
Lives a koala, fluffy and shy,
With fur as soft as cotton,
And a round nose, not forgotten.
His big fluffy ears,
And big fluffy tail,
Make him look so cute,
And never fail.
He munches on leaves, all day and night,
And takes a nap, when everything's alright,
He's a sleepyhead, and likes to nap,
But when he's awake, he'll climb and clap.
He's a curious creature, and loves to explore,
But always comes back to his eucalyptus bore,
With his eucalyptus leaves, he'll stay,
And all his needs, it will allay.
He's a protector of his home,
And will defend it, when he's alone,
He's a symbol of peace and tranquility,
A being of serenity, and pure humility.
He's a gentle animal, with a gentle pace,
And a peaceful demeanor, he'll never replace,
He's a friend to all, and loves to share,
His home in the eucalyptus, with those who care.
So, if you ever come across a koala,
In the eucalyptus trees, up high,
Don't be afraid, he's just a cute,
And fluffy animal, that just wants to be nice.
With his soft fur and gentle ways,
He'll steal your heart, in so many ways,

A true symbol of the Australian wild,
A koala, cute, fluffy, and mild.
He's a true wonder, of the wild,

The Race of the Grasshoppers

In the meadow, green and bright,
Lives a tribe of grasshoppers, ready for a race,
With legs so strong and wings so light,
They're ready to take flight.
They gather round, and make a plan,
To hold a race, and see who can,
Jump the farthest, and fly the highest,
In this race, they'll be the wisest.
The race begins, with a hop and a leap,
The grasshoppers jump, with a beep and a peep,
They jump and fly, with all their might,
To be the winner, they'll put up a fight.
They jump over flowers, and through the grass,
They fly over bugs, and surpass,
They use their wings, to soar and glide,
In this race, they'll be the guide.
The finish line, is in sight,
And with one final jump, they take flight,
They cross the finish line, and raise their legs,
The winner of the race is who beg.
The tribe cheers and jumps for joy,
For the winner, they'll be the toy,
They'll give him flowers, and a crown of leaves,
For winning the race and achieving the feat.
The race is over, but the fun isn't done,
They'll hold another one, under the sun,
For the grasshopper tribe, loves to race,
And in the meadow, they'll always be in first place.
So, if you ever come across a race,
Of grasshoppers, in a meadow, with grace,

Don't be surprised, it's just their way,
To have fun and enjoy the day.
With their legs so strong, and wings so light,
They'll jump and fly, with all their might,
A true symbol

The Honeybee's Labor of Love

In the garden, where the flowers bloom,
Lives a hardworking honeybee, who's met with gloom,
The task at hand, is one of great toil,
To gather nectar, and make honey, is her royal foil.
She flies from flower to flower, with great care,
Collecting nectar, with her proboscis, to repair,
The colony, which depends on her,
For food and survival, she is the purr.
She works all day, without any rest,
For the colony, she'll do her best,
With determination, and perseverance,
She'll gather nectar, with great endurance.
The honeybee is diligent and true,
For her colony, she'll always do,
She'll work hard, and never say die,
For the colony, she'll always try.
She'll fly from flower to flower, with ease,
Collecting nectar, as the colony increases,
She'll return to the hive, with her load,
And share it with the colony, for them to behold.
The colony, will work together, to make,
The nectar, into honey, for the colony's sake,
They'll store it, in the honeycomb, with care,
For the colony, they'll always be there.
The honeybee is a symbol of hard work,
For the colony, she'll never shirk,
She'll gather nectar, and make honey,
With diligence and determination, she'll never be sunny.
So, when you see a honeybee, flying by,
Remember her hard work, and try not to sigh,

For she works hard, to keep the colony alive,
And her hard work, will always thrive.
As the seasons change, and the flowers bloom,
The honeybee will be there, with her broom,
To sweep away, the nectar and pollen,
And bring it back to the colony, as a token.
The honeybee's hard work, is never done,
For the colony, she'll always run,
With diligence and determination,
She'll always be the colony's foundation.
Her hardworking nature, is one to admire,
For the colony, she'll never tire,
She'll gather nectar, and make honey,
For the colony, she'll always be sunny.
So let us all, take a leaf out of her book,
And work hard, without a second look,
For hard work, is the key to success,
And the honeybee, is the embodiment of this progress.
With her wings and her proboscis,
She flies and collects, with love and with focus,
She works tirelessly, day in and day out,
For the colony, she will never have any doubt.
The honeybee, is a symbol of hard work,
Diligence and determination, she will never shirk,
She'll fly with grace and poise,
And never make any noise.
She'll gather nectar, and make honey,
For the colony, she'll never be sunny,
For she is the foundation of the colony,
And she'll always be there, with her humility.
So let us all, take a leaf out of her book,
And work hard, with determination and a second look,

For the honeybee, is a role model,
For us all, to follow.

The Inquisitive Meerkat

In the golden sands of the savannah,
Lives a creature small and nimble,
With eyes that sparkle and a nose that wiggles,
The curious meerkat is always on the lookout for a gamble.
With its head held high, it surveys the land,
Searching for the next thing to explore,
With a keen sense of smell and a quick-witted hand,
It's always ready to open a new door.
It digs and burrows, it climbs and scurries,
An expert in the art of survival,
With a heart full of curiosity and a mind that worries,
It's always on the lookout for a rival.
It's a friend to the birds, a foe to the snakes,
A protector of its family and its kin,
With a courage that never falters and a spirit that never breaks,
The meerkat is always ready to begin.
It's a symbol of hope, a beacon of light,
A reminder of the power of the small,
With its curious eyes and its inquisitive might,
The meerkat stands tall.
So let us take a moment to admire,
The curious and inquisitive meerkat,
For in its quest for knowledge, it never tires,
And its spirit is forever intact.

The Fish of Many Colors

In the depths of the ocean blue,
Lies a world of wonder and surprise,
Where the colors of the coral and the creatures,
Are more vibrant than the bluest of skies.
And among these rainbow hues,
Swims a fish that stands out from the rest,
With scales that shimmer and shine,
It's the true rainbow of the coral crest.
The tropical fish, so small and bright,
With a tail that flows like a flame,
It dances and glides through the water,
A true work of art, without any shame.
It's a symphony of color,
A masterpiece of nature's design,
With hues of red and orange,
And a touch of yellow that truly shines.
It's a creature of the coral reef,
A part of the ocean's grand scheme,
With a heart that beats with wonder,
And a spirit that is truly serene.
For in the coral reef,
Lies a world of beauty and grace,
And the tropical fish,
Is a shining star in this underwater place.
So let us take a moment to admire,
The colorful and vibrant tropical fish,
For in its rainbow of hues,
Lies a true oceanic bliss.

The Lagoons' Jewel

In the salty marshes and lagoons,
Lies a creature of beauty and grace,
With legs as long as a willow's branch,
And a neck that stretches to trace.
It's a bird of elegant design,
With feathers as pink as a rose,
And a head that holds a crooked beak,
And a heart that truly glows.
The flamingo, so tall and thin,
With a stance that's truly grand,
It stands on one leg with poise and ease,
And surveys the land.
It's a bird of many mysteries,
With a life full of wonder and surprise,
It's a creature of the wetlands,
And a true beauty of the skies.
With a dance that's slow and fluid,
It wades through the shallow waters,
With a rhythm that's both hypnotic,
And a grace that truly matters.
For in the wetlands,
Lies a world of beauty and peace,
And the flamingo,
Is a shining star, that will never cease.
So let us take a moment to admire,
The graceful and elegant flamingo,
For in its pink plumes,
Lies a true avian halo.
It's a bird of elegance and poise,
With a spirit that's truly divine,

It's a creature of the wetlands,
And a true ambassador of the brine.
With a life that's full of mystery,
And a heart that's full of fire,
The flamingo is a true wonder,
A bird that will always inspire.
In the salty marshes and lagoons,
The flamingo will always reign,
With its pink plumes, and elegant stance,
It will forever remain.

The Unstoppable Beaver

In the deep and darkening woods,
Lies a creature of strength and skill,
With gnarled and nimble paws,
And a heart that beats with will.
It's a rodent of great renown,
With a talent for building and craft,
And a tail as flat as a paddle,
And a spirit that's truly daft.
The beaver, so strong and steady,
With a work ethic that's truly grand,
It toils away with tireless effort,
And shapes the land.
It's a creature of many talents,
With a life full of labor and pride,
It's a builder of the wilderness,
And a true expert in the tide.
With a gnaw that's sharp and fierce,
It fells the trees with ease,
With a determination that's truly peerless,
And a strength that will never cease.
For in the woods,
Lies a world of toil and strife,
And the beaver,
Is a shining star, that brings new life.
So let us take a moment to admire,
The hardworking and tireless beaver,
For in its dam,
Lies a true engineer.
It's a creature of industry and craft,
With a spirit that's truly divine,

It's a builder of the wilderness,
And a true expert in the brine.
With a life that's full of labor,
And a heart that's full of fire,
The beaver is a true wonder,
A rodent that will always inspire.
In the deep and darkening woods,
The beaver will always reign,
With its dams and lodges,
It will forever remain.

The River Rascal

In the sparkling rivers and streams,
Lies a creature of joy and glee,
With sleek and shiny fur,
And a playful energy.
It's a mammal of great delight,
With a talent for swimming and play,
And webbed and nimble paws,
And a heart that's full of sway.
The otter, so playful and sprightly,
With a spirit that's truly grand,
It frolics away with tireless energy,
And shapes the land.
It's a creature of many talents,
With a life full of laughter and fun,
It's a builder of the wilderness,
And a true expert in the sun.
With a dive that's bold and fearless,
It swims the rivers with ease,
With a determination that's truly peerless,
And a grace that will never cease.
For in the rivers,
Lies a world of play and mirth,
And the otter,
Is a shining star, that brings new birth.
So let us take a moment to admire,
The playful and energetic otter,
For in its slide,
Lies a true lover.
It's a creature of joy and laughter,
With a spirit that's truly divine,

It's a builder of the wilderness,
And a true expert in the brine.
With a life that's full of play,
And a heart that's full of fire,
The otter is a true wonder,
A mammal that will always inspire.
In the sparkling rivers and streams,
The otter will always reign,
With its slides and burrows,
It will forever remain.
With its playful antics,
And its gleeful chatter,
The otter is a true treasure,
A creature that truly matters.
So let us raise a cheer,
For the river rascal of the wild,
The playful and energetic otter,
A creature that's truly mild.

The Ocean Jester

In the vast and mighty ocean,
Lies a creature full of cheer,
With a coat of fluffy fur,
And a playful spirit dear.
It's a mammal of great grace,
With a talent for swimming and play,
And flippers that are nimble,
And a heart that's full of sway.
The seal, so playful and sprightly,
With a spirit that's truly grand,
It frolics away with tireless energy,
On the ocean's shifting sand.
It's a creature of many talents,
With a life full of laughter and fun,
It's a master of the waves,
And a true friend of the sun.
With a dive that's bold and fearless,
It swims the seas with ease,
With a determination that's truly peerless,
And a grace that will never cease.
For in the ocean,
Lies a world of play and mirth,
And the seal,
Is a shining star, that brings new birth.
So let us take a moment to admire,
The playful and energetic seal,
For in its slide,
Lies a true appeal.
It's a creature of joy and laughter,
With a spirit that's truly divine,

It's a master of the waves,
And a true friend of the brine.
With a life that's full of play,
And a heart that's full of fire,
The seal is a true wonder,
A mammal that will always inspire.
In the vast and mighty ocean,
The seal will always reign,
With its slides and burrows,
It will forever remain.
With its playful antics,
And its gleeful chatter,
The seal is a true treasure,
A creature that truly matters.
So let us raise a cheer,
For the ocean jester of the wild,
The playful and energetic seal,
A creature that's truly mild.

The Fluffy Hopper

In the meadows and the fields,
Lies a creature full of grace,
With long ears that flop and wiggle,
And a smile that lights up the place.
It's a creature of soft fur,
With a tail that's round and white,
And a nose that's always twitching,
In the morning's early light.
The rabbit, so cute and fluffy,
With a spirit that's truly sweet,
It hops the fields with joy,
On a journey that can't be beat.
It's a creature of many talents,
With a life full of fun and cheer,
It's a master of the burrows,
And a true friend to all that's dear.
With a journey that's carefree and light,
It hops the fields with ease,
With a determination that's truly bright,
And a grace that will never cease.
For in the meadow,
Lies a world of green and gold,
And the rabbit,
Is a shining star, that never grows old.
So let us take a moment to admire,
The cute and fluffy rabbit,
For in its journey,
Lies a true treasure.
It's a creature of cuteness and fluff,
With a spirit that's truly divine,

It's a master of the burrows,
And a true friend of the vine.
With a life that's full of joy and laughter,
And a heart that's full of cheer,
The rabbit is a true wonder,
A creature that will always be dear.
In the meadows and the fields,
The rabbit will always hop,
With its joy and its laughter,
It will forever find a top.
With its cute antics,
And its fluffy chatter,
The rabbit is a true delight,
A creature that truly matters.
So let us raise a cheer,
For the fluffy hopper of the wild,
The cute and fluffy rabbit,
A creature that's truly mild.

The Kangaroo's Odyssey

In the land down under,
Lies a creature full of glee,
With legs that are strong and bouncy,
And a tail that's long and free.
It's a creature of great power,
With a pocket that's warm and snug,
And a face that's always smiling,
In the bright and shining sun.
The kangaroo, so playful and energetic,
With a spirit that's truly wild,
It jumps the land with grace and ease,
On a journey that's never mild.
It's a creature of many talents,
With a life full of fun and cheer,
It's a master of the outback,
And a true friend to all that's dear.
With a journey that's full of adventure,
It jumps the land with pride,
With a determination that's truly admirable,
And a grace that's hard to hide.
For in the land down under,
Lies a world of red and gold,
And the kangaroo,
Is a shining star, that never grows old.
So let us take a moment to admire,
The playful and energetic kangaroo,
For in its journey,
Lies a true story.
It's a creature of strength and power,
With a spirit that's truly divine,

It's a master of the outback,
And a true friend of the vine.
With a life that's full of joy and laughter,
And a heart that's full of cheer,
The kangaroo is a true wonder,
A creature that will always be dear.
In the land down under,
The kangaroo will always jump,
With its joy and its laughter,
It will forever find a bump.
With its playful antics,
And its energetic chatter,
The kangaroo is a true delight,
A creature that truly matters.
So let us raise a cheer,
For the jumper of the wild,
The playful and energetic kangaroo,
A creature that's truly mild.

The Octopus' Odyssey

Deep in the ocean's depths, where the sun's rays cannot reach,
Lives a creature most peculiar, with eight arms that each can teach.
A mollusk of great intelligence, with a mind that's sharp and sly,
The octopus is an expert in disguise, who can change its colors in a
sigh.
It can squirt ink to escape its foes, or blend into the sea,
With its ability to adapt and change, it's truly wild and free.
It can open jars and solve puzzles, with its suction cups so fine,
Its curiosity and problem-solving skills are truly one of a kind.
It's a creature of great mystery, with a life we still don't know,
But one thing is for sure, the octopus is an expert in its own show.
It's a creature of great beauty, with its colors so vibrant and bright,
It's a curious and inquisitive being, that's truly a wonder to sight.
So next time you're diving deep, and you see an octopus' form,
Remember the mind that lies within, and the many ways it can
transform.
For in the ocean's depths, there's a creature most peculiar,
The octopus, a being of great curiosity and wonder.
The octopus is a creature of many talents, with an inquisitive mind,
It can swim, crawl, and even fly, as it explores the sea to find.
It's a solitary creature, who roams the ocean's vast expanse,
And with each new discovery, it's given a chance.
To learn and grow and adapt, to the changing sea and land,
The octopus is always searching, for the next thing to understand.
It's a creature of great resilience, who can survive in the harshest of
conditions,
With its ability to adapt and change, it's truly a master of evolution.
The octopus is a creature of great intelligence, with a brain that's truly
unique,
It's a master of problem-solving and can even learn to speak.

It's a creature of great creativity, who can build and create,
With its eight arms, it can shape the world, and make it truly great.
The octopus is a creature of great beauty, with its colors so vibrant and bright,
It's a symbol of the ocean's diversity, and a wonder to sight.
So next time you're diving deep, and you see an octopus' form,
Remember the mind that lies within, and the many ways it can transform.
For in the ocean's depths, there's a creature most peculiar,
The octopus, a being of great curiosity and wonder.
A creature that inspires us to explore and learn,
And to never stop searching, for the answers that we yearn.

The Busy Bee's Labor

Amidst the flowers, in fields of green,
A hardworking bee is rarely seen.
But listen close, and you'll hear the hum,
Of a tireless worker, never done.
With wings a blur, and legs a-dance,
She darts and dips in her bee-like prance.
Collecting nectar, and spreading pollen,
She works with purpose, never slacken.
The bee's labor is never done,
For there's always more flowers to be won.
She'll fly for miles, and brave the heat,
To bring back sweet nectar, so delicious and sweet.
But her work is not just for herself,
For her hive and colony, she works with stealth.
She'll gather and store, with care and might,
To ensure the survival of her kin, day, and night.
So next time you see a bee at work,
Remember the labor and toil, the endless perk.
For without the tireless bee,
The flowers would wilt, and the world would be incomplete.
The bee's tireless labor, a reminder to all,
Of the value of hard work, and the importance of small.
She will fly in the morning and fly in the night
She will fly in the rain, and she will fly in the light
She will work hard to make sure her colony survives
For a bee's work is never done and it never thrives
She will gather nectar and pollen and bring it back home
She will make sure the hive is never alone
She will take care of her queen and her drones
She will make sure that the hive is always grown

She will defend her hive with all her might
She will fight off any enemy in sight
She will protect her kin with all her might
For a bee's love for her colony is always bright
So next time you see a bee flying by
Remember the hard work and the never-ending try
For without the tireless bee, the world would not be the same
For the bee is the one who brings sweetness and fame.

The Hedgehog's Curiosity

In a small burrow in the ground,
Lived a hedgehog, small and round,
With quills that prickled to the touch,
And a curious mind that loved to hunch.
He'd explore the forest and the field,
His nose always to the ground, sealed,
In search of bugs and tasty treats,
His hunger for adventure never depletes.
He'd climb trees and slip through the brush,
His senses always on the hush,
For he knew that danger lurked nearby,
But his curiosity could not be denied.
He'd watch the bird's fly overhead,
And the squirrels gathering acorns to be fed,
He'd listen to the crickets sing,
And to the bees buzzing on their wing.
He'd come across a stream and dip,
His toes in the cool and clear water, a sip,
And watch the fish swim lazily by,
His mind filled with wonder and sigh.
One day, as he was exploring the land,
He came across a strange and unusual band,
Of creatures he'd never seen before,
With tentacles that reached to the shore.
They were octopuses, hiding in the sand,
Their colors changing to blend in, grand,
And the hedgehog's curiosity was sparked,
As he watched them move and work.
He watched as they used their tentacles,
To catch their food and defend,

And he marveled at their intelligence,
Their adaptability, immense.
From that day on, the hedgehog knew,
That there was so much to explore and pursue,
And he set out on a journey, anew,
To discover all the world has to do.
His curiosity had led him to new heights,
And he now saw the world in new lights,
With new friends and new adventures,
His life was filled with new endeavors.
So, if you ever come across a hedgehog,
With quills that prick and eyes that jog,
Don't be afraid, for he's just like you,
Curious and inquisitive, with so much to do.

The Backwards-Hopping Kangaroo

n the land down under, where the sun is hot,
There lived a kangaroo, who was quite the trot.
He hopped and leapt with pride,
Through the bush and the fields, his joey by his side.
But one day, as he hopped along,
He stumbled and fell, with a great big thong.
He looked back and saw, to his surprise,
That he had been hopping backwards with his eyes.
He tried to hop forward, but found it hard,
His body just wouldn't move, it was quite bizarre.
He tried and tried, but to no avail,
He couldn't hop forward; it was quite a fail.
He felt quite down, and quite depressed,
His joey tried to cheer him, but he couldn't be impressed.
He thought his life was over, it was quite a plight,
To be a kangaroo who couldn't hop right.
But then one day, as he lay in the shade,
He saw a group of kangaroos hopping in a parade.
They hopped and leapt, but to his surprise,
They hopped backwards before their eyes.
He realized then that it was okay,
To hop in his own way.
He practiced and practiced, and soon found,
That hopping backwards was quite profound.
He could hop over obstacles with ease,
And surprise others, with his newfound skills with such breeze.
He was proud of himself, and his unique hop,
And his joey was proud too, for he never stopped.
And so, he hopped, through the bush and the fields,
With his joey by his side, and his heart full of zeal.

He was a kangaroo like no other,
Who learned to hop backwards, like no other.
And from that day on, he was known,
As the backwards hopping kangaroo, who had grown.
Into a confident, self-assured marsupial,
Who hopped to the beat of his own drum, with no denial.

The Sloth Who Dreamed of Speed

In the lush jungle, where the leaves rustle,
There lived a sloth, who hung from a bustle.
He was slow and steady, and content with his pace,
But deep down inside, he longed to race.
He looked at the monkeys, as they swung from tree to tree,
And envied their speed, so wild and free.
He watched the birds, as they soared through the sky,
And dreamed of the day when he could fly.
He lay in his tree, and closed his eyes,
And imagined himself, running with the guys.
He saw himself, racing through the jungle,
With the wind in his face, and his heart in a jumble.
He dreamed of the day, when he could be fast,
And leave behind, his slow and steady past.
He longed to be like the others, who could move with ease,
And not be defined, by his slow disease.
He tried to force himself, to move faster,
But his body just wouldn't comply, it was quite a disaster.
He grew frustrated, and felt quite low,
For he knew that his dream, would never come to fruition, and never
grow.
But then one day, as he lay in his tree,
He heard a wise old owl, speak to him with glee.
The owl said, "My dear sloth, you must learn to see,
That true strength and beauty, come from being true to thee."
The sloth thought about this, and realized with a smile,
That he was special, and unique, and that's worthwhile.
He was proud of his slowness, and learned to embrace,
The beauty of moving at his own pace.
And so, he hung from his tree with grace,

Content in his slowness, and with a peaceful face.
He knew that he would never be fast,
But that was okay, for he was true to himself at last.
He watched the monkeys, as they swung from tree to tree,
And the birds, as they soared through the sky,
And was happy for them, and their wild speed,
But was content to live his life, at his own unique pace indeed.
And from that day on, he was known,
As the wise old sloth, who had grown.
Into a happy, content marsupial,
Who lived his life, at his own pace, with no denial.

The Love of a Porcupine

In a forest, deep and dense,
Lived a porcupine, quite immense.
He had quills that were sharp and strong,
But his heart was warm, and he loved to belong.
He roamed through the woods, with a smile so wide,
Hoping to hug and be by someone's side.
He hugged the trees, and the bushes too,
But they couldn't hug back, and he knew it was true.
He hugged the birds, and the bees,
But they flew away, with a buzz and a breeze.
He hugged the deer, and the bears,
But they ran away, with a startled stare.
He didn't understand why they couldn't see,
The love and affection, that he wanted to be.
He felt so alone, and quite low,
For he just wanted to give hugs, and to show.
But then one day, as he lay in the grass,
He met a skunk, who was small but so crass.
The skunk said, "Porcupine, why do you hug,
When all you do is just scare and bug."
The porcupine thought about this, and felt quite confused,
For all he wanted, was to be loved and used.
He realized then that his quills were sharp and strong,
And that they could hurt if he hugged for too long.
He made a decision, to hold back his embrace,
And instead, to show love, with a kind face.
He smiled and waved, and let out a squeak,
And found that friendship, was just within reach.
He met a raccoon, who was shy and meek,
But with a smile, they became friends in a week.

He met a fox, who was cunning and sly,
But with a wave, they became friends by and by.
He learned that love, doesn't have to be hugged,
But can be shown, in many different ways, be it with a wave or a shrug.
He learned that his quills, can be both a blessing and curse,
But with a kind heart, they can be a positive force.
And so, he roamed, through the forest once more,
Showing love, with a smile, an open heart, and a warm core.
He may not have hugged, as much as before,
But he knew that true friendship, is something worth fighting for.
And from that day on, he was known,
As the porcupine, with a heart of stone.
Into a kind and loving creature,
Who lived his life, showing love in his own unique feature.

The Bat and the Firefly

In a cave, deep and dark,
Lived a bat, with a heart so stark.
He had wings that were strong and black,
But his fear of the dark, was a constant attack.
He fluttered in the cave, with a heart full of dread,
Hoping to escape, the darkness ahead.
He avoided the shadows, and the corners too,
But the darkness always seemed to pursue.
He avoided the night, and the dusk as well,
But the darkness, seemed to cast its spell.
He felt trapped, and quite low,
For he just wanted to escape, the darkness that he knew.
But then one day, as he hung from the roof,
He met a firefly, who was small but so proof.
The firefly said, "Bat, why do you fear,
The dark when it's a part of your dear."
The bat thought about this, and felt quite confused,
For all he wanted, was to be free and used.
He realized then that his wings were strong and black,
And that they could fly if he just got back.
He made a decision, to embrace the dark,
And instead, to explore, with a fearless spark.
He flew into the shadows, and the corners too,
And found that the dark, was not so scary, after all, it was true.
He met an owl, who was wise and meek,
But with a smile, they became friends in a week.
He met a fox, who was cunning and sly,
But with a wave, they became friends by and by.
He learned that the dark, doesn't have to be feared,
But can be explored, with a curious mind and a heart that's cleared.

He learned that his wings, can be both a blessing and curse,
But with a fearless heart, they can be a positive force.
And so, he flew, through the cave once more,
Embracing the dark, with a curious mind and a fearless core.
He may not have feared, as much as before,
But he knew that true freedom, is something worth fighting for.
And from that day on, he was known,
As the bat, who once had a heart full of stone.
Into a curious and fearless creature,
Who lived his life, embracing the dark in his own unique feature.

Ismael S. Rodriguez Jr., also known as The Bulletproof Poet, is a talented and diverse artist, writer, and poet of Puerto Rican and Filipino descent. He was born and raised in Philadelphia, PA, and now lives in Oakland Park, FL. Rodriguez has a range of interests and experiences, including serving in the U.S. Navy and being deployed during Desert Storm. Despite facing numerous challenges in his life, including schizophrenia, substance abuse, and homelessness, Rodriguez has overcome these obstacles and has been sober for 15 years. He is also actively seeking treatment for his mental and emotional health. In addition to his artistic pursuits, Rodriguez is an ordained reverend and practices Grey Witchcraft, Discordianism, and ceremonial magic. His website, https://thebulletproofpoet1.godaddysites.com/home, showcases his poetry, short stories, origami, and more. You can find additional links to his work on his Linktree https://linktr.ee/bulletproofpoet or contact him directly at Ismael@bulletproofpoet.com.